j
Nash, Renea D.
Coping as a biracial/biethic
teen

D0345480

PoN

ALLEN COUNTY PUBLIC LIBRARY
FORT WAYNE, INDIANA 46802

You may return this book to any agency, branch,
or bookmobile of the Allen County Public Library

7/98

DEMCO

FUNDS TO PURCHASE
THIS BOOK WERE
PROVIDED BY A
40TH ANNIVERSARY GRANT
FROM THE
FOELLINGER FOUNDATION.

C OPING

AS

A Biracial/

Biethnic

Teen

Renea D. Nash

THE ROSEN PUBLISHING GROUP, INC./NEW YORK

Published in 1995 by The Rosen Publishing Group, Inc.
29 East 21st Street, New York, NY 10010

Copyright 1995 by Renea D. Nash

All rights reserved. No part of this book may be reproduced in any form without permission in writing from the publisher, except by a reviewer.

First Edition

Library of Congress Cataloging-in-Publication Data

Nash, Renea D.
    Coping as a biracial/biethnic teen/Renea D. Nash.—1st ed.
    p.   cm
    Includes bibliographical references and index.
    ISBN 0-8239-1838-6
1. Children of interracial marriage—United States—Juvenile literature.   2. Teenagers—United States—Life skills guides—Juvenile literature.   3. Ethnicity in children—United States—Juvenile literature. [1. Interracial marriage. 2. Life skills. 3. Conduct of life.]   I. Title.
HQ777.9.N37   1994
306.84'6—dc20   94-22140
                                       CIP
                                       AC

Allen County Public Library
900 Webster Street
PO Box 2270
Fort Wayne, IN 46801-2270

Manufactured in the United States of America

To Mycah, Leah, Sarah, Connie, Nancie, Jillesa, Arielle, Marette and Brigetta—a few of the many beautiful biracial people in this world. And to my niece, Eunice Nicole.

Renea Denise Nash was raised in Saginaw, Michigan. The youngest of five children, she found her privacy by writing her thoughts in journals and turning her feelings into poetry. Occasionally, she sang to express her emotions, but she was a much better writer.

She received a bachelor's degree in journalism from Central Michigan University in 1986. After working for newspapers in Maryland and Ohio for two years, Renea headed for Phoenix in search of warmer weather. There, she worked for corporate newspapers and award-winning magazines. She works in the public relations field and continues to free-lance as a writer.

In 1993, she earned a master's degree in mass communication from the Walter Cronkite School of Journalism and Telecommunication at Arizona State University, where she was also named the school's outstanding graduate. Her first book, *Coping with Interracial Dating*, was published in May 1993.

Contents

Introduction

We live in a society that simplifies complicated racial equations into basically six categories: white, black, Asian, Hispanic, Native American, and other. If your mother is Native American and your father is Hispanic, it's clear what *they* would mark. If your mother is black and your father is Asian, it's clear what *they* would mark. What do you, the child with a dual racial heritage, mark?

Some people believe that biracial children should choose between their races because it would be impossible for them to maintain a dual relationship to both racial groups. They say that choosing one would mean rejecting one half of a person's heritage. Would it or wouldn't it?

According to books on the subject of biracial children, parents tend to deal with the racial and ethnic identity of their children in one of three ways: Some parents say that their child is a human above everything else—that color is totally irrelevant; other parents teach their children to take on the identity of the parent of color and to learn minority survival skills; the third group teaches their children that they are biracial and should have a biracial identity. Which group do your parents fall into? Which do you think is best for you? Have you and your parents discussed your racial identity?

These are some tough questions and issues, and you're at the age now when you're either getting a little tired of answering the question "What are you?", marking the "other" box, or marking just one box. Your identity is not about what other people want to know about your racial background or how society categorizes you, is it? It's about you. It's about who you are.

You may find it comforting to know that there are about five million biracial citizens in this country. Although most statistics and published materials talk about black/white unions, the racial combinations of biracial individuals are endless! For example, Japanese-Americans marry non-Japanese-Americans about sixty-five percent of the time. The number of babies born in the U.S. with one Japanese and one white parent has exceeded the number with two Japanese parents since 1981. These figures and the ones below come from a special issue of *TIME* magazine on "The New Face of America." In fact, population experts predict that by the year 2000 minorities will begin to be the majority.

Seventy-six percent of the population in 1990 was white, twelve percent black, nine percent Latino, and three percent Asian. By 2050, the breakdown is projected to be: white, fifty-four percent; black, sixteen percent; Latino, twenty-two percent; and Asian, ten percent. Unfortunately, predictions for multiethnic Americans were not included. But be assured, this group is on the rise as well.

So don't ever feel that you're all alone in your experiences as a biracial child. Many biracial teens are living through the same challenges. Regardless of their particular backgrounds, biracial people have a common bond that links them to similar prejudice, stares, and questions. It also links them to something unique: a true cultural experience.

Most biracial children grow up to be happy, healthy adults, with a good outlook on life. That might be hard to believe. But now that you're older, be aware that the debate over how biracial children's identities should be developed and supported is hot!

Maybe you're saying to yourself, "I don't have any problems. I know who I am. What's the big deal?" Well, you're smart enough to know that you don't necessarily have to have a problem. It's the other people who may have a problem about you or your parents. It wasn't too long ago—about 1967—that the Supreme Court finally struck down existing state laws against interracial marriages. The obsession with race is still going on and will probably do so for some time.

Here's another example: Did you know that there are various viewpoints on the terminology to be used in describing biracial people? There's **interracial, biracial, mixed, brown, multiethnic, multiracial, mulatto, multicultural, bicultural, and rainbow**. You may even know of a few more, not including the cruel names some people may have called you. This book will use many of the terms throughout, but you will find interracial and biracial to be the most commonly used. The use of these terms in no way discounts the ongoing discussion of terminology; it's simply what the author feels is less confusing for you, the reader.

But let's get something straight about a few terms: race, ethnicity, and culture. The word race implies a biological distinction among people, based on physical characteristics, and classifies us accordingly. The most commonly distinguished races include caucasoid, mongoloid, and negroid. However, it's no longer that simple. Distinguishing groups by skin color is.

Ethnic is defined as "of, pertaining to, or designating races or groups of races on the basis of common traits, customs, etc." Today we expand this to refer not to only racial traits, but to national, tribal, religious, and linguistic traits as well. The major ethnic groups in the U.S. are Irish, Italian, Polish, Jewish, Chinese, Japanese, and Hispanic. Except for Jewish people, the above names refer to the nationality of origin. Judaism is a religion; therefore a Jewish person could be black, white, Chinese, Peruvian, etc.

Culture is the "act of developing by education, discipline, training, etc." This process takes in the customary beliefs, social forms, and material traits of a group.

The classifications used to describe people and their races and cultures are confusing. People are reexamining and redefining these descriptions to get rid of misleading and prejudiced language. Some social scientists would rather not use the word race. Instead, they suggest that people be thought of in terms of their ethnicity. In this book, we'll refer to racial and ethnic groups to include everyone.

In the next hundred pages, you'll read about how other teens feel about growing up as biracial children and how most of them feel they have the best of two worlds. You'll read about the concerns and issues your parents faced when they decided to have children. You'll read about the importance of racial and ethnic identity and how our society is beginning to celebrate diversity.

These are tough chapters with a lot of information, so be sure to read them a little at a time. You'll read about how our society categorizes people, then freaks out because the process is really not as simple as "check one." One chapter talks about couples adopting children outside of their race in what is referred to as "transracial" adoptions. You'll find stories created to illustrate the point made in the chapters.

At the end of the book, you'll find a list of various support groups, books, and publications that are directed toward you—the biracial individual. Please consider this a chapter to read carefully, rather than "the references in the back of the book" because it's important that you and your parents do the suggested reading. You'll find the information very valuable and useful. For example, without the assistance of the Biracial Family Network of Chicago, I wouldn't have been able to research this topic thoroughly. The kind people there sent me many articles and a list of hundreds more!

Support is out there when you need it, want it, and look for it. It's as close as your own home because this book is also for parents and brothers and sisters. Think about the questions I ask throughout. Think about each situation and ask yourself, "How would I have reacted?" Take from it whatever is useful to you. Read the entire book. Read it twice. I hope you enjoy it. I hope you tell others about it.

CHAPTER 1

Growing Up Beige

"**P**eople always ask me, 'What are you?'"

It's not the usual question teenagers are asked, but Connie has grown accustomed to the fact that when she walks into a room full of strangers or attends a new school, the question is going to be asked. After one glance at her long, wavy, light brown hair and beige complexion, it would be a matter of seconds before someone inquired about her racial identity.

"I'm black and Italian, I tell them," Connie says. "I hate the way they ask, 'What are you?' That sounds so stupid."

"Taking care of my hair. When I come out of the shower, I have a big afro."

For Melissa, a seventh-grader, grooming her thick hair—which is too long and frizzy to wear straight like the blond locks of her mother and too straight to wear short and kinky like her African-American father—is a real challenge. Although she struggles each morning to style her hair, the end result is a wonderful mane that is the envy of her female classmates. And that too is a challenge.

"People call you half-breed, zebra, salt and pepper, and polka dots, or oreo—because you're white and black," says Melissa.

Name-calling was part of childhood for Connie and Melissa. It's not so much a part of their lives now that they're teenagers.

Children who resort to this kind of name-calling have heard lots of discussion about race and have been influenced by what their parents and friends say, and by the media.

"Sometimes I feel I don't fit in with my classmates because I don't speak Japanese, although I'm half Japanese."

Kim, the son of a Japanese mother and a white father, doesn't want to be left out of the Japanese culture because his family speaks English instead of Japanese in their house, or because he's never been to Japan. The Asian students at his school think Kim is more American than he is Japanese. They treat him like an outsider, because to them he is "not Japanese enough."

"I love being biracial. I understand and get along with both races."

Leah, the teenage daughter of a black/white couple, views the world through both her father's brown eyes and her mother's blue eyes. She celebrates having the best of both worlds.

"My parents raised me to be proud of who I am, and I am. The benefits of having both cultures far outweigh anything bad I experienced in growing up."

Nancie, who's half Mexican and half white, can't imagine being anything but biracial. She can't wait until she has children of her own to pass on her dual cultures.

"Sometimes I check the box marked 'other' just to mess with people. I mean, I'm not an other. If I can't mark the boxes for both Hispanic and black, then I usually mark black. Sometimes I mark only Hispanic. It just depends on what mood I'm in."

Debra is a self-proclaimed radical. She knows that even if officials created a "mixed" or "multiethnic" category for her to check, it wouldn't end racism.

When schoolchildren who belong to the dominant culture learn that someone is biracial or mixed—of at least two different races—they react as they do to other things that are unfamiliar to them. They turn on an internal coping device that helps them accept things that are unfamiliar to them. Laughter and name-calling are just two ways some choose to cope. Some choose to ignore or reject one part of you. For example, how many times have you heard a racist joke about your race? What happens? The person telling the joke, realizing that you may be offended, says, "Oh, I don't mean you."

Tactics like these make them feel better, but how does the person on the receiving end of such unhealthy tactics cope? How do you cope with being a biracial teen?

Growing up is not easy to begin with. All children go through a period of feeling left out, unpopular, or as if the whole world's against them. Parents refer to it as a phase that will pass. It does, usually. It also usually recurs during adolescence and passes again.

But when you grow up as a biracial child your life can be more challenging. For example, a child of some intermediate shade, having parents of different complexions, is often questioned about race and identity. Isn't it unfortunate that a little girl of beige complexion is questioned about her skin tone with comments like, "Your mother must let you play too long in the sun"? Isn't it enough sometimes to make you want to scream? Go ahead. It's actually good for you. Bottling up your anger only leads to stress.

Let's talk about identity. Biracial offspring don't have a clearly defined and quickly categorized identity. People like to think in absolute terms. "What are you?" To that question, people expect a simple answer: African-American, white, Hispanic, Japanese, Italian, Native American, Arab, Puerto Rican, and so forth. They don't want to accept, "Half this, one-quarter that." How can this be? Which one are you? To choose or not to choose? That is the question.

The day you were born, your parents had to make a decision about what to write on the forms to describe your racial identity. Some parents choose to use the race of the parent of color as identification. Some people try to buck the system and put down both races. Often, this is met with, "You can't do that," from the nurse. What did your parents choose for you? Is that what you call yourself today?

Some biracial teens are rejected by people of both the races of their parents, or accepted by one and rejected by the other. They are thus discounted, if you will, because they are not "pure" anything. But is there any such thing as pure, really? Ask someone you think is one hundred percent black. You'll probably find that somewhere in that person's family tree is some Native American, Spanish, or German ancestry. Ask someone who you think is one hundred percent anything and listen to the response. The United States is rapidly becoming a nation of multiethnic people. For example, the National Center for Health Statistics reports that the number of babies born to white mothers and black fathers rose from 7,244 in 1968 to 33,875 in 1988. The number of babies born to black mothers and white fathers rose from 2,375 in 1968 to 17,070 in 1988.

Over a period of two decades, the number of interracial marriages in the U.S. has escalated from 310,000 to more than 1.1 million.* The incidence of births of mixed-race babies has multiplied twenty-six times as fast as that of any other group; the number of Jews marrying out of their faith has shot up from ten percent to fifty-two percent since 1960; about sixty-five percent of Japanese-Americans marry people who have no Japanese heritage; Native Americans marry out about seventy percent of the time; and the number of children born to these last groups exceeds the number born into uniethnic homes. And let's not forget about the couples who have babies but don't get married.

The size of the multiracial population is estimated to be five million, according to the Biracial Family Network in Chicago. Just take a look at some of the famous movie stars and celebrities who are from mixed heritages: actresses Rae Dawn Chong, Jasmine Guy; singers Prince, Mariah Carey, Paula Abdul, and Vanessa Williams. Hollywood is full of multiethnic Americans, and so is the rest of our society. The exact number of the multiracial population is unknown. Why? Because when the government takes the census every ten years, it requires people either to identify with one race or ethnic group or to check "other."

Unfortunately, our country seeks to oversimplify complicated racial equations to either "black" or "white."

* *TIME* magazine, 1993

But where do you fit in if your mother is Asian and your father is white? Or if your mother is white and your father is Hispanic? Or if your mother is Native American and your father is black? Or any combination of the many racial identities in our world? Where do you belong if you don't fit into one category, if you don't fit into one box? Well, in the eyes of the government officials, you have to choose just *one* to belong to.

Does that mean you can be Native American on one government form and white on another? Do you see the contradictions? There are many multiethnic Americans and parents of mixed children who are pushing for new census categories that will allow people to be very specific about their racial and ethnic identities. You'll read about this in a future chapter.

Acceptance by our peers is something that is important to all of us, no matter what age or what race we are. We all want to be liked, loved, embraced, part of the crowd— accepted. Some people go to extremes to be accepted. For some biracial people, the need for acceptance is over-whelming. Gaining acceptance may mean denying their true racial heritage, pretending to deny it, or trying to act more like one race than the other, to fit in. What do you think of that? Is that what you're doing? Do you feel that you are forced to live under false pretenses?

Even when biracial individuals are embracing both their racial identities equally, they are often accused of trying to be more of one race than the other. Why would some-one accuse them of that? Ever heard of the green-eyed monster called jealousy? He has the knack of rearing his ugly head, and he can live in all of us. Kermit-the-frog sings, "It's not easy being green." The lesson to learn from this Muppet is that it's not always easy living in a world where you're either this or that when you're neither.

This first chapter is an overview of the subject of biracial and multiethnic identity. What is it like growing up as a biracial child in a world so obsessed with color that some people are paralyzed by the hatred sent their way? Only multiethnic Americans truly know the answer to that question. But in these pages we'll talk more with some of the teens introduced at the beginning of this chapter and explore how other biracial teens and their parents answer questions about their racial identity. You'll learn why it's important to develop a strong identity and celebrate diversity.

For now, meet Brittany Saddler. She lives with her parents and her younger brother, Zach. Her father is African-American and her mother was born in Germany, where she spent most of her childhood. They live in a middle-class neighborhood. Brittany is a sophomore in a predominantly white high school. Let's see what growing up beige has been like for Brittany and Zach.

Five years ago Brittany's father was transferred to California. It was the third time her family had pulled up stakes since she was five years old. Last week, she turned sweet sixteen and was given a surprise party by her friends. It was a great party, and everyone was in the family room dancing to the sounds of Michael Jackson and eating pizza. She finally felt as if she had somewhere to call home. But on Friday, December fourteenth, her father called a family conference in the very room where they had celebrated her birthday and his promotion. This was to be their last Christmas spent in sunny Anaheim. Their new home would be in Brentwood, Tennessee.

"I have some great news and some not so great news," her father had announced. "Which would you like to hear first?"

"The great news!" Brittany's eight-year-old brother exclaimed. Zach was what Brittany called an eager beaver. Everything in life was exciting to him.

"OK, the great news it is," her father went on. Brittany's mom had obviously heard the news already, because she was all smiles. But there was a strain in her smile, and her green eyes told Brittany that the not-so-great part of the news was really bad news.

"Well, kids, I've been promoted. You're now looking at the senior vice president of human resources for Alcoa," he said proudly.

"Yeah!" Zach jumped for joy. Then he stopped with a puzzled look on his face. "What does that mean, Daddy?"

"It means we're moving again, doesn't it, Daddy?" Brittany interjected in a sharp tone. Her "Daddy" was not as full of affection as Zach's was. Her mother's smile disappeared. "Doesn't it?"

"Hold on, young lady, watch your tone of voice," her father demanded. "Zach, it means that Daddy will be in charge of a lot of people and making a lot of money."

"All right, we're rich!" Zach yelled.

Brittany's father paused before continuing. He looked at his daughter, who was now sitting with her arms folded in front of her, impatiently waiting for the answer she knew was coming. "And yes, it also means that we'll have to move to be near the corporate offices in Brentwood, Tennessee."

"Tennessee?" Brittany hated the South. Anything east of California and south of Chicago was a hick town to her. She was a metropolitan teen who loved city life. "This is a joke, right? Please say you're joking." Tears had formed in her eyes. Her voice was trembling.

"Sorry, Brit, I'm not joking," her father tried to calm her. "I know we've moved quite a bit, but this is it. I promise that this will be our last move until you are both out of high school."

"That's great news, Rod, honey," said her mother, trying to relieve some of the tension in the room. "I'm sure the kids are proud of you, aren't you, Brittany and Zach?"

"Way to go, Dad!" Zach shouted.

Brittany said nothing.

"The cat got your tongue, Brittany?" Zach prompted her to speak.

She finally did, softly and slowly. "Of course, I'm proud of you, Daddy—but the kids here finally accept me." Then she became frantic. One would have thought she had just received the death penalty, the way she carried on. "I don't want to do it all over again," she yelled. "I just can't! I won't!"

Brittany ran out of the room as fast as her legs would take her. She was in tears.

"What's wrong with Brittany?" Zach asked his parents. "Why is she crying?"

Brittany's mother looked at her husband. He gave her a nervous glance in return.

Zach was eager as usual for an answer. "What's wrong, I say!" he shouted, nervously.

"Calm down, Zach," his mother replied, patting him on the head. "We'll talk to you about why Brittany's upset."

His father took over the conversation. The transition was so smooth, it was like watching a tag team wrestler take over in the ring when one can no longer handle the pressure. They had obviously been planning this discussion for some time.

"When your mother and I were dating, people looked at us kind of funny. Do you know why?"

"Yeah," Zach replied quickly, to his parents' surprise. "Because of your bald head!"

"Well, that's probably one reason, but the other one is because your mom and I are of different races."

Zach examined both of his parents' faces quickly. "You mean because Mom is a Nazi?"

This shocked both Mr. and Mrs. Saddler. They had never used the word around their children. They tried not to show their discomfort.

"Where did you hear that, Zach?" his father asked calmly.

"From this kid in school," he said. "I told him that Mommy was from Germany and this new kid, Casey, he's sort of the class clown, he moved here from someplace called The Hood, the teacher is always yelling at him, we all laugh at him. Casey said that people who came from Germany are Nazis. What's a Nazi?"

Zach's father wanted to hear more about this street-wise kid Casey. "What does Casey say about me, Zach?"

"Oh, nothing much. He says you're an Uncle Tom, and sometimes he calls me Zach-the-Zebra."

At that, Mrs. Saddler could no longer stand up. She plopped down on the sofa.

"Zach, why haven't you ever told us about what this Casey boy says?" his mother inquired.

"Uhh, . . . uhh," he said in a very small voice—the tone he used when he thought he had done something wrong and was about to get into trouble.

"It's OK, Zach, we're just asking," she comforted her son.

"It's not OK, Brigetta." Mr. Saddler was obviously upset. "We can't let kids fill his head with nonsense about you being a Nazi and me being an Uncle Tom. My God! This Casey kid is only nine. Where does he get this stuff?"

"Now, Rod, you know Casey learned it from his parents."

"Why are parents feeding kids this garbage? I don't tell my kids that all whites are prejudiced and that we blacks should revolt. And I, of all people, have the right to be angry."

"Why? Why, Rod?" Mrs. Saddler questioned, rather loudly. "Because of something that happened long before you were born? Is that where you get this so-called right? Is that the way you live, in the past?"

"No, of course not," he answered, just as loudly. "But I'm sick and tired of always defending who I am, who my kids are and how I got here. I've worked hard to get where I am, and I didn't get here being anybody's Uncle Tom. If I want to marry a white woman and have kids, that's my business," he continued with the same energy Zach often used. "And if I want to marry a Martian and have half-green kids, that's my business too!"

"What's going on, and what's wrong with Zach?" a voice came from the doorway. It was Brittany. The yelling had interrupted her sulking.

Her parents were so busy with their own discussion, they had forgotten about Zach, who had now crawled under the glass coffee table. He was crying.

"Oh, Zach," his mother reached for him. He pulled back. "Come here, honey. We're sorry. We didn't mean to upset you."

"Who's having green kids?" Brittany asked.

The room fell silent. It was broken by Mrs. Saddler's laughter. "Your father was making a point," she said.

Brittany was confused. "I don't get it."

"Let's all sit down and get our bearings." Mrs. Saddler motioned the kids to the sofa. Mr. Saddler began speaking.

"Kids, I know we're not what society considers to be the average American family. And I know sometimes the kids at school tease you about having parents of different races and being the color that you are—kind of beige, I guess."

"Like the sofa!" Zach interjected.

His father glanced at the leather sofa. "Yeah, I guess, kind of beige like the sofa," he answered. "But that doesn't mean you're different or weird or should have to accept any verbal abuse from anyone or be treated differently by your teachers or your schoolmates.

"Be proud. You have the opportunity to enjoy the richness of two cultures," he continued. "I've always taught you to be proud of both your heritages and ignore what other people say."

"You mean Casey?"

"Yes, Zach, people like Casey," his mother responded. "Although Casey learned those things from his parents."

"Will it always be this way for us?" Brittany asked. "Will I always have to explain to people what I am?"

"Who knows?" her father answered. "Right now, the kids in your school have accepted you as a hip teenager, one who happens to have parents of two different races." Brittany smiled at her father's outdated lingo. "The kids in Tennessee will also discover how hip you are," he said confidently. "In the meantime, you go on being Brittany."

"And I'll be Zach!"

"Yes, that's right, son," Mr. Saddler said, giving Zach a big bear hug. "It's a crazy world we live in. People are so obsessed with color." He paused. "Brigetta, remember when you tried to register Brittany in preschool?"

"Yes," Mrs. Saddler laughed. Her husband joined in with her.

"Tell me! Tell me!" Zach was his old self again.

"What happened? You never told us that story." Brittany was almost as excited as Zach.

"Well . . ." Mrs. Saddler began, still laughing. "The

lady at the desk took one look at me and one look at that beige skin of yours and asked, 'What race is your daughter?' I said, 'She's half African-American and half German.' The lady looked confused, and said, 'So is she black or white?'"

"And I looked back at her, and said, 'I told you, she's half and half.' The lady was getting upset with me and replied, 'Would you say she's more black or more German?'"

"That's stupid," Brittany interjected.

"Yes, it was," her mother agreed, still laughing. "I couldn't get it across to this lady that you were equally African-American and equally German, and probably a little bit of other races, since none of us were pure anything. Finally, I told her to give me the form."

Her father continued from there. "Your mother took the form and where it asked you to fill in race, she put in H-U-M-A-N, and told the lady, 'Miss, my daughter is a member of the human race. How's that?'"

Everyone laughed until their sides ached, especially Brittany, since the story was about her.

"When will this madness over color end?" she asked.

No one could give her an answer.

"Well, until it does, and since I'll have to be going through this madness again in good ole Brentwood, Tennessee, I'll probably need something to help me cope . . . and since we're going to be rich and all, Dad, how about a convertible?"

Laughter again filled the Saddler house, and this time it was Brittany's father who laughed the loudest.

Brittany asked a good question: When will this madness over color end? You, the biracial child in a society still obsessed with color, may have to lead the way to change.

CHAPTER 2

Developing Racial
Identity

W hen you were a very young child, playing with the other kids in your neighborhood, you probably didn't think of them as being of any particular color or race. They were just your play-mates, the kids you hung out with until the porch light came on. It's not that you didn't realize you were all of different racial backgrounds, but playing and having fun was the focus of your attention. By the age of seven or eight, most children are well aware of their ethnic labels: "I'm African-American," "I'm Japanese-American," "I'm Mexican," and so forth.

Many sociologists and social psychologists have researched and studied the development of ethnic identity beyond childhood years. They did so by using Asian, African-American, and Chicano people as examples. People in these ethnic groups as well as others such as Native American, Puerto Rican, and Hispanic, are considered to be in the minority. White people of European descent are considered to be in the majority.

The researchers came up with a series of steps that minority people take as they adapt themselves to the white society. Most agree that this process occurs early in adolescence: the teenage years. So on top of dealing with normal teenage things, minority teens go through an additional growing phase.

Certain things happen that force minority teens to reexamine the meaning of their ethnic identity. Minority teens start thinking, "What does it mean to be black? Hispanic? Cambodian? Puerto Rican?" As they mature, and their cognitive abilities increase, they become better able to understand their experiences in society. They have increased interactions outside their own community, and this enables them to compare the differences between themselves and others.

For example, when you hang out with people of another race you notice some of the things they do differently from members of your race or culture. It seems that many white kids like rock and roll or country music and many African-American kids prefer hip-hop. This has a lot to do with the music business, and target marketing.

Another thing that happens during their teen years is that people become more interested in their appearance, dating, and thoughts about their future. "What career path do I want to follow?" "Whom will I marry?" Researchers believe these are the things that shape the way minority teens develop their individual identities.

Developing your racial identity is important for you. Reading about it here will hopefully clear up some of the problems you may be experiencing. Take your time . . . read this chapter twice if you like. You'll learn a lot.

Racial identity is defined as "pride in one's racial and

cultural background." It's important to develop a strong racial identity for several reasons. According to the professionals, it is crucial because it helps clarify your attitudes about yourself, about other individuals in your racial/ethnic group, about other ethnic minority groups, and about people in the dominant culture.

There is a myth that all individuals from a particular minority group are the same and have the same attitudes and preferences. You've probably heard comments like, "All black people can dance" or "All Japanese people are smart."

In 1983, two social scientists formulated what they called the Minority Identity Development Model. They described the various stages that people go through as they formulate their personal identity with regard to race. The model includes a stage having to do with *conformity*. In this stage, minority people accept the values and attitudes of the dominant culture and internalize the negative viewpoints directed at the minority culture. These people may even fantasize about being white in an attempt to distance themselves from the minority race.

Another stage is identified as the *crisis*. Here, minority individuals experience a growing awareness that not all the cultural values of the dominant group are beneficial to them. The crisis occurs when these people experience prejudice against different skin colors.

Another stage is that of *exploration*. Some psychologists refer to it as the immersion stage because in it the minority individuals search for a better understanding of themselves and their people. For example, in this decade, many African-Americans have started to identify with the customs, attire, and hairstyles of "the motherland."

Another stage is the one in which minority people finally *identify with* and commit to their own particular group.

If you've read carefully, you've probably picked out a few things that didn't sit well with you, a person with two racial identities. One psychologist, W.S. Carlos Poston, Ph.D., took a look at the model, and said, "This doesn't work fully for a biracial individual."

First, he said, the model implies that individuals choose one group's culture or values over another's. He also noted that the model suggests that minority individuals first reject their minority identity and culture and then accept the dominant culture. Biracial children, he points out, may come from both of these groups. How can you reject one but accept the other when you belong to both?

Poston points out that the model does not allow for you to have several different racial identities at the same time. It suggests that you can reach self-fulfillment only when you integrate yourself into one racial/ethnic identity and reject all the others. In other words, based on the stages described, Hispanic people could be secure in their identity only if they accepted the fact that they belonged to the Hispanic culture and accepted and followed the traditions, customs, and values of that—and only that—culture. But what if these Hispanic people were half Hispanic and half white? The model doesn't work for them.

Finally, Poston points out other problems with the model. It requires that the minority person be accepted into the minority culture. This, he said, does not always happen for biracial people. Many biracial people are not accepted into their parents' cultures—whether they be minority or dominant. For example, a black/Asian child may not be accepted by the Asian side of his or her family. In fact, biracial persons experience more prejudice than anyone else.

Although most biracial families claim having the best of

both worlds, another model, the Marginal Person Model, introduced by E.V. Stonequist, suggests that people of mixed races are associated with both worlds but do not wholly belong to either. Stonequist suggests that for these people there is uncertainty and ambiguity in identification with parents, peers, and society.

In other words, he thinks that being biracial causes problems in developing a truly integrated self-image. He says such a person is not able to fit in anywhere. He is not alone in this thought. It's likely that your parents were cautioned about bringing mixed kids into this world. "What about the children?" is usually the first response from people who think like Stonequist.

Poston says that the major flaw in this Marginal model is that it wrongly places the identity problems on the biracial child. Poston argues that the lack of support that some biracial people receive from their parent cultures is the real cause of their difficulties.

Poston believes it is possible for biracial individuals to exhibit characteristics of both cultures without having the so-called problems suggested by the Marginal Person Model. All they need is loving support from both their parent cultures.

Before we continue, let's review. We've learned that developing one's racial identity is connected with having pride in both parental cultures. We've learned that this pride helps shape attitudes about oneself and others. We've learned that developing one's racial identity does not happen overnight; it happens in stages. We've learned that people do not allow for unique racial mixtures. We've also learned that biracial individuals can exhibit characteristics of both cultures without conflict.

Poston developed his own five-stage model, which he described in the November/December 1990 issue of the *Journal of Counseling & Development*. His stages include: *personal identity, choice of group-categorization; enmeshment/denial; appreciation;* and *integration.*

In the first stage, *personal identity*, the individual is often very young and just becoming aware of belonging to a particular ethnic group. The child tends to have a strong sense of self—based on self-esteem and feelings of self-worth developed and learned in the family—that is, independent of ethnic background. Basically, this is just a happy kid who enjoys playing with other happy kids. In the second stage, *choice of group-categorization*, individuals are pushed to choose an identity, usually of one ethnic group. This can become a time of crisis and alienation. Does the question, "What do you consider yourself?" sound familiar? Some pro-fessionals have found in talking with biracial adults that they felt as if society had forced them to make a specific racial choice in order to participate in society. One teen who is half Italian-American, half black-Puerto Rican was asked, "If there were a war between blacks and whites, which side would you be on?" Perhaps the correct response would be, "I'd try to make peace between the two."

During this identity crisis, professionals say, biracial people have two choices. One is to choose a multicultural existence, which includes the racial heritage of both parents; the other is choose one parent's culture or racial heritage over the other. Several factors govern the choice: status, social support, and personal issues.

Do you live in a middle-class suburb with predominantly white neighbors, or do you live in the inner city among the working class? Issues of status arise here.

Matters of social support arise out of the following considerations. Are your parents high-school educated or college graduates? What about your grandparents; do they accept your interracial family? Then there are personal factors such as your age, your physical appearance, being bilingual, how much you know about the cultures in your background, your political involvement, and your individual personality. Are you willing to learn your parent's native tongue? All these thing play roles in helping biracial individuals understand and formulate their own racial identity.

A young man who is African-American and German may identify himself as black because his skin color is closer to black than white, because he grew up in a predominantly black neighborhood, and because his German mother's parents wouldn't accept a "black" grandchild. Poston thinks, and you may not agree with him on this one, that it would be unusual for teenagers to choose a multiethnic identity. You must decide this for yourself.

The third stage, *enmeshment/denial*, brings about confusion and guilt at having to choose only one identity, one that is not fully expressive of one's background. People may experience bouts of guilt and self-hatred. They may also be rejected by groups that they seek to join. One social psychologist has found that a multiethnic child who is unable to identify with both parents has feelings of disloyalty and massive guilt over the idea of rejecting one parent. For example, a biracial teen may be ashamed and scared to have friends meet the parent whose racial background is different from that of most people in the neighborhood; and he or she may feel guilty and angry for feeling this way. What happens? Eventually, the teen has to learn to appreciate the cultures of both parents or stay at this level emotionally. Parental and community support is crucial in helping the biracial child resolve this dilemma.

The *appreciation* stage follows: the embracing of one's multiple identity. Biracial individuals at this stage begin to learn about their racial/ethnic heritage and cultures, but they still tend to identify more strongly with one group. (The choice they make is influenced by the factors mentioned in stage two.) The person we talked about earlier who identified himself as black might still seek knowledge of his German ancestry and participate in German cultural activities.

The final stage Poston identifies is *integration*. At this stage, biracial individuals experience wholeness and belonging. They recognize and value all of their ethnic heritage: They are secure in who they are. One study conducted in 1980 found that sixty-seven percent of all the biracial adults were at this level. That should tell you that if a multicultural existence is what you want, you can have it and enjoy it.

Poston's model is similar to the others, but it introduces several important issues and assumptions. Let's go over them. This model brings out the fact that biracial individuals tend to have identity problems when they internalize outside prejudices and values.

Biracial people may experience alienation and make choices they are uncomfortable with. Choosing one affiliation over another can result in feelings of guilt and disloyalty to one of the parents.

Integration is healthy. The most difficult times of adjustment and confusion are during the choice phase and the enmeshment/denial phase. If you are experiencing this now, just remember that you're not alone in the world. It's very important to seek support from parents, siblings, and support groups.

You may accept all of what Poston has said here, some of it, or none of it. Remember, this is just one person's theory, and it needs to be tested and examined over and over again. As mentioned at the beginning of this book, and what will be a theme throughout, the issue for biracial individuals of developing one's racial identity is not black and white. There are many gray areas that still lead to much debate. Counseling sessions are now available for biracial adolescents. In a paper titled *Identity and marginality: Issues in the treatment of biracial adolescents*, a psychologist identifies issues and problems she has worked with that may or may not come as a surprise to you. They include: identity confusion, self-hatred, substance abuse, suicide, delinquency, alienation, denial of self, gender identity confusion, and feelings of guilt and disloyalty.

Counselors can help biracial teens in many ways. They can help cope with the problems that come with being biracial or multiethnic by helping you understand that you may be internalizing negative attitudes about your cultural background. They can:

- provide a safe atmosphere in which you can express feelings of anger and alienation
- provide names of support groups in the area
- provide materials to help you learn about your parent's ethnic or cultural group or even discuss with you the benefits of adopting a biracial identity.

They can also help your parents to help you. Chapter 3 talks more about what your parents can do.

Finding a counselor if you choose this route is something you and your parents must do carefully. Often there are counselors at school. The counselor or therapist you and your family select to help you with identity development must have examined his or her own feelings and attitudes about interracial marriages and biracial persons and learned about a wide variety of cultures.

Remember, many, many biracial teens have handled their biracial identity development successfully without professional assistance and have grown up to become happy individuals. These adults say that their parents facilitated their healthy self-concept by giving them love and support, while at the same time providing them with the knowledge of both—or all—of their racial/ethnic identities and emphasizing the positive aspects.

So never underestimate the power of looking for support right at home. You will find that your parents can help you, and you can help them too.

CHAPTER 3

Baby Makes Three

Families come in all sizes. On the one hand, you have the "Brady Bunch" family complete with mother, father, kids, a maid and a dog. A good storyline for television, but pretty far from reality for most people. On the other hand, you have a "Thea" or "Blossom" family with a single parent raising three children. Also situation comedies on television, but a little closer to real families of the 1990s. A single man and his pet are a family too.

Families also come in many forms. Two people who have a child together but never marry are a family. Two people who adopt a child are a family. Children who live in foster homes have foster families. A divorced man and his children are a family.

Families come in many colors. Your family is living proof of that statement. For any family, no matter the size, form, or color, the addition of a baby is challenging. Some people challenge the family portrait created by interracial families, which adds additional pressure to their lives. Most stories interracial families tell are positive, but some are not.

Some interracial couples face discrimination when trying

to rent or purchase a place to live. Some couples report the loss of friends and cold treatment by their families and their coworkers. Some even report receiving poor service in restaurants and theaters. Most give accounts of stares, whispers, and questions. You can see that your mother and/or father had some coping of their own to do.

Television, motion pictures, and even Broadway plays have shown interracial and intercultural relationships for decades. "Guess Who's Coming to Dinner," "West Side Story," "Jungle Fever," "Not Without My Daughter," all depict the outcome of forbidden love just as in Shakespeare's "Romeo and Juliet." "All in the Family," starring Carroll O'Connor as Archie Bunker, does an excellent job of showing what prejudice is.

"I Love Lucy," starring red-haired Lucille Ball and Cuban-born Desi Arnaz as husband and wife, went on for more than a decade without problems, even when Little Rickie, the couple's biracial child, was born. The show touched on cultural and language barriers the couple had to deal with daily.

But that's television.

Imagine being thirty years old, newly married, and about to have your first baby. It's probably very difficult for you to think that far ahead right now. But try to imagine the excitement of the young couple who are about to bring a new life into the world. Debra and Bill Gebhardt didn't have to imagine this excitement; they lived it. In April 1989, Debra was rushed to the hospital delivery room at the same time her husband was rushing their taxes off to the post office to meet the IRS deadline. Fifteen hours later, a bouncing baby girl screamed her arrival.

Debra and Bill, an interracial couple, were now a family of three. They called their daughter Jillesa. "The little child looked white," Debra laughs, "and here I am, black as black can be."

Since this was their first child, the young couple didn't know what to expect. They also didn't expect what happened the next morning. When Jillesa was born, an identification bracelet was attached to her wrist and a corresponding one attached to Debra, identifying her as the mother. At feeding time the next day, Debra says, a nurse entered her room with the baby but stopped at the door, turned, and took the baby back out. The nurse returned moments later with a puzzled look but no infant. Debra says the nurse walked over to the bed, checked Debra's ID bracelet, and returned to the hallway, where a ten-infant caravan of newborns awaited delivery to proud mothers along the corridor. The nurse returned once again with the baby, but the puzzled look had not left her face. She held the baby's tiny wrist next to Debra's and checked the numbers—twice. They matched. She relinquished the baby to Debra. It was a ritual the new mother became familiar with. Other mothers and fathers of biracial children have also reported having their biological bond to their children questioned.

"They'd come into my room, and they'd look at me and leave, then they'd go look at the baby, then they'd come back and look at me," Debra laughs. "They'd check her ID; then they'd check my ID. But if my husband Bill was in the room, they'd only check a couple of times. If he wasn't there, they'd check and check and check because they didn't believe she was my baby.

"She looked really really white," Debra says of her daughter, who now has a beautiful beige complexion. "It was really hard on me. I would say, 'Give me my child, please!'"

Even when she and the infant arrived home, her

parenthood was questioned—this time by the friend of a friend. Seeing Debra holding the infant close to her bosom, the guest asked if she was baby-sitting.

"I didn't know what she meant," Debra says. "'No,' I said, 'this is my baby.' No one wanted to believe Jillesa was my baby because she was so white. It took her a long time to get darker. I was worried. My husband and my brother kept telling me not to worry. I don't know why I was worried; I just wanted her a little darker."

Now the mother of three beautiful girls, Debra compares their features to one another. Arielle has more black features, according to Debra. "Look at her nose," she says as she looks at her middle child. "Her face is black, but her skin is not as dark. Jillesa has more white features, like Bill, with that nose and the thin lips." The third child, Marette, has black features so far.

After a while, Debra gave up the color game she caught herself playing. "I don't care how dark or how light they are—as long as they're healthy," she says.

Debra's humor and candidness are healthy signs that she has always been very comfortable with her interracial family. "I just thought we were going to have kids," she says. "We didn't think about whether they were going to look black or white."

For many young couples in love, the question of having children is often asked in terms of, "Are we financially ready?" Other concerns, especially for those in interracial alliances, often come from outsiders. It wasn't until 1967 that the U.S. Supreme Court struck down state laws banning interracial marriage in the case of *Loving v. Virginia.*

For Debra and Bill, the apprehension over having children was first expressed by Bill's parents, who were against the marriage from the beginning. In fact, the grandparents were never informed that their grandson was seriously dating a black woman. Debra and Bill wed in secret. When Bill's parents found out about this, they immediately turned their anxiety to the thought of having biracial grandchildren.

"She thought biracial children wouldn't have a chance in life. I really don't know what else she thought, but the instant she found out she was a grandmother, she changed totally," Debra recalls, adding that in the past Bill's mother had threatened to disinherit him.

Debra theorizes that her mother-in-law's apprehension stemmed from the fact that she lived in a small white community where there were very few minority families—and no interracial couples. Also, Bill's grandparents, who come from a strict German family, were from the old school, where white was white, black was black, and no one crossed the color line. They had passed along their ideas of separatism to their daughter. This is not a suprising transference, since professionals say that pre-judice starts at home and is taught right along with the ABCs and the 1-2-3s. Like any other learned behavior, it can be unlearned.

Now that Bill's grandparents have died, Bill's mother has begun to think on her own, says Debra. "She just had to change her thinking about it . . . and she has. She loves these kids."

When asked whether she and her husband have to explain to the children about their racial makeup, Debra relates a story. Debra, a school teacher, ran across multi-cultural crayons by Crayola on a shopping excursion for classroom supplies. The crayons offered a variety of colors resembling skin tones. She bought them for her class and her children.

One day Jillesa, the oldest child, had forgotten her

skin-tone crayons at her grandmother's house, so she drew a family picture without them. Jillesa colored her mother with a black crayon. However, her sisters and father were left the color of the paper, white. "Mommy's black, that's why I colored her black," she told a visiting cousin.

"At one point, when she was three, Jillesa thought she was white, and I told her she wasn't," Debra says. The young child had come to that conclusion after comparing her skin to her parents'. Since her skin looked more like her white father's, she asked if she was white.

"I said, 'No, you're not, you're considered black. You're a light-skinned black. You're part black and part white, but we would call you black.'"

But why? Why does Debra consider her biracial child to belong to only one race? Other parents do the same. "Because when you're asked on forms, there's no category for them," Debra explains. "There's black, white, Hispanic, Native American, but no 'other' or no 'none of your business.' I would check that: none of your business."

For some parents of interracial children, checking the "other" box is viewed as having no category at all. While the Gebhardts seem happy and well able to cope with life as an interracial family, Debra may be viewed by some other parents of biracial children as being too complacent or too passive in her response to the way society views her children, or in the way she handles questions of their identity.

There are so many concerns about how to help biracial children grow up healthy and happy, and a lot of these concerns are in the area of language and terminology. That is, what words do we use to describe people's ethnic and racial makeup? Many viewpoints were expressed by parents and scholars at a 1984 conference in New York City where the needs of interracial families were addressed. It was the first of its kind. Sponsored by the Council on Interracial Books for Children, the conference included a series of presentations and panel discussions devoted to the development of positive self-identity in interracial children and to the need for the creation of resources that reflect the reality of our interracial society.

Although those who gathered for the conference came with a variety of viewpoints and questions, the overriding concern then (as today) was the following: How do parents of interracial children raise normal, healthy children in a society that views interracial unions as abnormal and harmful?

When dealing with human factors, nothing is simple. All interracial families want to be treated like normal families, but as one parent said at that conference, "We are not the problem, but because society sees us as a problem, it creates problems for our children."

Your parents may be struggling with some of the very issues that you're trying to deal with as a biracial child. Do you talk with your parents about your racial duality? Parenting isn't easy: Babies don't come with instructions. Sure, Dr. Spock may offer some insightful remedies for bedwetting, but the kinds of pressures society places on parents of interracial children are difficult to handle.

Other concerns surfaced at that historical conference and were highlighted in the *Interracial Books for Children Bulletin*, a publication produced by CIBC. Conference participants often spoke about the fact that interracial or multicultural families are virtually invisible in literature, curricula, and the media. The lack of support, materials, and information for interracial families appears to be a constant issue. Think about it: When was the last time you opened a storybook or a textbook and found a family like yours? Wouldn't such books be helpful in generating discussions around issues of racism and cultural differences? Storybooks about the hurt of racism or about mixtures within the emerging American families could create a climate for discussions in which biracial children could work through their feelings. Reading stories about young people like you or parents like yours, no matter what your racial or cultural heritage, would help you validate your uniqueness and promote self-esteem. On page 115 is a list of the few books available in your public library that pertain to or include interracial families. Why not write a children's book of your own? This would be especially rewarding if you have younger siblings who will travel the same road you're traveling now.

Let's turn now to racism. Although the last legal restrictions to interracial marriages in the U.S. were struck down in 1967 by the Supreme Court, racism is still the force behind the problems that interracial couples and their children have—no matter what their racial mixture. It is within the context of U.S. racism that interracial children struggle to form a sense of identity.

In the *Bulletin* article, "Interracial Children: Growing up Healthy in an Unhealthy Society," the author makes the point that racism has led to our society's "limited and irrational" definition of race. Here's how it works: Children with one white parent and one parent of color are generally identified one hundred percent with the parent of color, and their biracial identity is ignored. Children with one black American parent and one parent of a Third World background usually are perceived as black; in most cases, their biracial identity is also ignored by the wider society.

Scholars and parents alike agree that all interracial children must cope with racism affecting every child of color. More simply put, they are likely to face the same racist attitudes that minority children face. In addition, they say, children such as yourself must deal with outsiders who view your normal, loving, strong family as pathological, unstable, and peculiar, and the basis of any problems you may have. Did you ever have to talk to a teacher or school social worker about problems you were having at school? Did the subject of your family come up? Did you think that your family makeup was a factor or not? If they're not educated to the contrary, professionals often view interracial children's problems as a result of the nature of their families. Because of the lack of support in this area, parents can also wrongly come to view all problems as race-related.

Parents who attended this conference believe that interracial children must also cope with a society that has set up white standards of beauty. Think about it: the Barbie Doll, Cindy Crawford, Richard Gere. This one-sided standard of beauty affects all children of color as well as all biracial children. It can be particularly painful for girls who have a strong attachment to their white mother but who don't have her blond locks or porcelain complexion. Have you ever been asked if you were adopted? Have people asked you why you don't look like your father or mother? Children want to identify with both their parents, and they are hurt by society's rejection of their racial duality even when parents constantly affirm their beauty.

Here is a conversation between a black woman and her biracial child as told by the mother in an article in a 1992 *Glamour* magazine.

"Your skin is brown, right, Mommy?" the daughter said.

"That's right, my skin is brown," the mother replied.

"I wish you were white like me," the little girl said.

Trying not to sound unnerved, the mother responded, "Your skin isn't white."

"Yes, it is," the child replied. "It's the same color as Daddy's. I don't want to talk about it anymore."

According to the mother, the racial issues that she and her white husband regularly confronted had left their daughter confused. Despite the mother's efforts to answer her daughter's questions, the terms black and white had come to signify more than shades of color to the child. That day, she had made her choice to be white despite the mother's subtle messages that being black was as good and as beautiful. For example, she affirmed the beauty of color every time her daughter pointed to white models in magazines and commented on their beauty. The mother would point to brown-skinned models and praise both models. Although the mother believes her daughter thinks of her as beautiful, she says that her daughter's love can't entirely offset the damage done by "Madison Avenue and its American ideal of what is attractive." Again, she's speaking of the white standards of beauty many of the parents talked about at the CIBC conference. The mother also talks about the "colorization of poverty."

Here is a young child who is being told essentially that black is beautiful, yet in her travels around the city images of blacks in poverty are all she sees. Do you think she wants any part of a reality that she identifies as being black in America? The mother in this article stated that life would have been easier on her child if she hadn't seen the impact being black has on the mother, in relation to the daughter. For example, the child has on several occasions been asked if her mother was the family house-keeper. In another example, the mother's parental connection to her youngest child, a son, was questioned. Remember Debra and Bill from the early part of this chapter? The same sort of "This can't be your child" incident occurred at a party with her other child—in front of her daughter. And in yet another example, a policeman stopped and questioned the black mother about being in an all-white neighborhood, which was her own.

The author wrote: "Because of scenes like these, I understand why my daughter told me that she was white, and why she wished that I were, too. She was wishing that I had a way to pass into the easy life as well; she could already see that life as a black woman is harder."

The article ends with a later conversation about the young child's skin.

"You're brown, right, Mom?" the child asked.

"That's right," the mother replied.

Her daughter held out her own arm. "But I'm brown . . . and white."

"Yes," the mother replied, hugging her daughter. "I guess that sounds right."

The mother was satisfied with this and said she hoped that time and love would make her daughter strong enough to bear any hurt that came her way. That hope is one shared by many at the CIBC conference: that time and parental love would help their children live healthy lives. Part of that parental love is giving their biracial children coping skills. Those at the conference and many psychologists believe that interracial children need the same coping skills that all children of color learn.

For example, how does a white woman who is a single parent help her Hispanic-white son deal with racism when neither she nor her son have the coping skills that minority people have developed? These parents face the same task all minority parents face: to make their children feel secure and loved and at the same time prepare them for the harsh reality of racism.

Keep in mind that most of the parents at this CIBC conference were members of black and white couples. Everyone's experience is different. But let's say there is a single white father raising the children he conceived with his black partner. According to other single white parents, they are fearful that their children's experiences with racism will lead them to hold a grudge against their nonminority parent, blaming the white parent for their difficulties. Such fears, if not dealt with, can keep parents from adequately preparing their biracial children for a society that is not colorblind.

What answers did the council receive from interracial adults on the panels? All agreed that they did not blame either of their parents for the times they had to struggle to defend their background while trying to develop a clear sense of themselves. The toughest times in their lives? The teenage years. The only resentments came from those panelists who felt that their parents hadn't given them a clear grounding in either culture. Panelists suggested that the white parents in the audience study racism thoroughly, in order to understand how it would impact on their children.

Communication is the key in interracial families, just as it is in any family. Reaching an agreement, or consensus, on the best approach to helping children develop their identity is unlikely. There are no cut and dried answers. But the reason for this chapter will perhaps be the key to your success. The reason is simple: You need to understand the dilemma parents confront, and parents need to understand those faced by their biracial children. You and your family should read this book together.

Here are a few suggestions about coping with your interracial heritage, given at the 1984 CIBC conference.

You and your parents can talk about them and see if any of these suggestions are helpful.

1. Parents should be comfortable about their own identity, and they should talk through issues relating to their children's identity—both between themselves and with their children.
2. Parents need to realize that they cannot completely understand the experiences of their children if they are not biracial themselves.
3. Parents must provide biracial children with an environment in which they can raise questions, express anger, and work through feelings that may seem to threaten the family's sense of security.
4. Parents must deal openly with racism.
5. Parents must prepare their children for negative reactions toward the interracial nature of their family.
6. Panelists said that living in a mixed community made it easier for them as biracial children to have friends of all races and become comfortable with a variety of children.
7. Parents should establish a local support group.

You may want to set up a support group made up of other biracial teens or join existing ones, enabling children to meet role models through participation in social activities.

Support groups are discussed further in Chapter 10. Here are a few simple steps for you and your parents to follow in setting up a support group. Post notices on community bulletin boards and in schools or churchs and synagogues. Place ads in the newspapers, talk to other teens, and contact a few of the interracial organizations for input and suggestions. Church, synagogue, or community centers often offer their meeting rooms free of charge. Once a support group is established, you may want to subscribe to the newsletters of other interracial organizations. As you gain experience, you can start your own newsletter.

Remember, ultimately you—the interracial child—are the one who decides your identity.

So far we've talked only about problems. Many studies, however, paint a very positive picture of interracial families and their biracial children. These studies come to the same conclusion: Most interracial children become healthy adults. Such studies as those of Drs. Alvin Poussaint and Philip Spivey have focused on interracial children from black/white unions. (Dr. Poussaint's name may be familiar to you if you ever watched "The Cosby Show." He's a consultant and has appeared on many talk shows, including Oprah Winfrey's, discussing this very issue. He is an associate professor of psychiatry at Harvard Medical School.) Poussaint and Spivey's studies indicate that interracial children tend to be achievers with strong identities, comfortable in predominantly white or black situations, proud of their mixed background, and tolerant of other people's differences.

Are these traits that you've noticed about yourself? Do you feel comfortable in settings where there are people of varied racial or cultural backgrounds? Are you always the one in your circle of friends who promotes the peace when racial clashes are discussed? If these traits haven't surfaced in you yet, they probably will, especially if you and your parents communicate openly and honestly about your racial identity.

Interracial children must work through the conflicts of

being mixed children in a society that theoretically promotes pluralism while rejecting interracial unions. That process will be easier if parents present the situation realistically and work with other parents to make institutions more responsive to their children's needs. Interracial children can grow to be strong adults with positive self-identities. Ultimately, however, the problems interracial children face will be solved only when racism no longer exists in our society. When will that happen?

Society is changing so that the minority population will soon be the majority. Racial identity may not be as much of an issue in the year 2000. In fact, parents such as Debra and Bill seem to be banking on just that.

Says Debra, "When they grow up, it won't be a problem. At least, I hope it won't be a problem for them. I think it'll work itself out." She then looks into the eyes of her oldest, five-year-old Jillesa. "I think it's kind of neat. I mean, they look at their daddy, then they look at their mommy . . . and we're two extremes. One is white as white can be, and the other is black as black can be—I think that's special."

And no parent, single, married, divorced, or widowed, will argue with that.

CHAPTER 4

Who Am I?

"**I** am not here to beg and plead with this racist society for a racial identity. I already have a place—an interracial place. I already have an identity—an interracial identity. I exist. I am real. I am here. And I no longer feel that it is so much my responsibility to remind society of these facts, as it is this society's responsibility to simply recognize me."

Raise your hand if the above sentiments expressed by Bess Martinson in 1979 are similar to what you're feeling right now as you try to cope with society's relentless questioning about your identity. "What are you?" "Are you mixed?" "Where do you fit in?" If you're like most biracial teens and adults, you're probably tired of hearing, responding to, ignoring, or defending any questions, comments, or insults about your racial heritage.

You may find comments about your identity even more frustrating and nearly unbearable if you and your family have not discussed your unique racial makeup and how society views your interracial family. The development of one's racial identity, the topic of Chapter 2, will be the key in dealing with your peers at school. Much of this chapter echoes Chapter 2, except that you'll find the writing less clinical.

Professionals say your parents play a major role in helping you answer the questions, "Who am I?" and "Where do I fit in?" Biracial teens and adults say that your parents can either prepare you, or fail to prepare you at all. Prepare you for what?

Well, let's start with the most asked question, "What are you?" Black? White? Yellow? Red? Labels do not describe the actual skin color of any person. There's no such thing as white skin. People categorized as white have skin tones ranging from light pink, or yellowish, to various hues of olive, beige, or dark tan. People categorized as black have skin tones ranging from ebony to ecru to pinkish shades, and so forth. Actual skin tones vary so much that these kinds of color labels are confusing as well as inaccurate. For example, a child labeled "black" may look at his or her skin and say, "But I'm brown." Color labels don't work for biracial individuals because society refuses to recognize the blending of colors. Instead, biracial people are sometimes forced to choose one identity over the other, which leaves one parent's heritage blotted out. Some biracial people choose; some choose not to choose.

Most biracial people want to find their own identity and not be forced to fit images that society has defined for them. In some interracial families, perhaps including your own, parents influence the decision. Some parents may insist that their interracial children are not being raised according to race or color, but simply as human beings. There is nothing wrong with this type of thinking because it is essentially true; you and all the other multiethnic/ multicultural individuals are humans just like everyone else. But is life really that simple? Can you be raised as merely human with no emphasis on your race or color? Many professionals—and biracial adults—say that adopting this idealistic notion is one way parents can ill-prepare their biracial children for the real world.

Most people are likely to agree that children need to be taught that being black or Japanese or Mexican is a matter of being proud of belonging to a cultural group. Having ethnic and racial pride helps in building defenses against the negative attitudes that exist in our society. Doesn't it make sense to instill pride in being black/Japanese or Hispanic/white or black/white, or of mixed cultures? Biracial people who grew up to be healthy adults say it's because they were taught that they had the best part of their mother's culture and the best part of their father's culture all rolled up into one. That's perhaps the best part of being biracial: You have the ability and the right to embrace or claim more than one culture. That's really who you are, isn't it?

Simply having an awareness of your parents' heritage is not enough. You have to experience the cultures that make up your unique racial heritage. You can gain that experience in many ways. You can learn about your ancestors by reading history books in your school or local library, by looking at old family photo albums, and by talking to grandparents and great-grandparents, who often make the best oral historians. For some biracial people, experiencing the cultures within them may mean learning to speak other languages, learning and practicing a variety of customs and traditions, and attending and participating in special events such as parades, dances, and fiestas that celebrate the uniqueness of cultures.

Parents can provide these kinds of experiences for you, or you can seek them out on your own. Experts as well as

other biracial people agree that it's healthier for you and
your family if these experiences are on-going and happen
as a family, beginning early in your childhood. If you
haven't been doing these things, you're probably thinking,
"I'm a teenager. It's too late." It's never too late. If you
and your family members haven't been experiencing
these kinds of activities, start now. There are many fun
things to do, and to participate in. Seek them out. You'll
be pleasantly surprised.

Once you have accepted each part of your racial heritage
and allowed each to become an active part of you and
your life—once you have achieved a sense of identity—
handling questions such as "What are you?" will be as
comfortable as answering "How old are you?" Although
you may have pride in your ethnic/racial makeup and are
comfortable with your racial identity, you will probably
still grow tired of answering the same old questions. That
may be something you'll just have to learn to live with,
because biracial adults are always questioned. It never
ends. And since it never ends, you may find that getting
upset or showing frustration over having to address your
racial identity again and again takes a lot more energy
than just simply answering the question—very assertively,
of course. "My mother is black, my father is white," or
"My dad is Chinese, and my mother is white. And I
consider myself both Chinese and white." Or if you
decide to choose one identity over the other: "My mother
is Hispanic and my dad is black. I consider myself black."
Just remember, when you choose, this question is likely
to follow: "Why did you choose one race over the other?"
If you choose to identify with one race over the over,
you'll have to be prepared to answer even more questions.
There is also the likelihood that one of your parents will
feel rejected. There's a chance that members of the race

with which you've chosen to identify won't accept you as legitimate.

That's why discussing your unique racial identity with your parents and other members of your family is so important. What do you discuss? Discuss the issues your mother and father faced when they were dating and when they decided to have you. Discuss parental concerns (especially if you come from a single-parent home, because that parent needs support too). Discuss race relations in our society. Discuss prejudice and racism, and how to respond to discrimination. Discuss how you should identify yourself at school on forms, if you should check one box or two or none. Discuss your own concerns, fears, or anxieties, if you have any. Discuss skin color, hair texture, and your other physical features. Discuss your feelings with your brothers and sisters and let them express theirs to you. In other words, discuss anything and everything you haven't discussed or thought you couldn't or shouldn't.

Every interracial family is different and handles its racial identity differently from other families. Racial identity may be handled differently even among members of the same family. For example, TV talkshow host Geraldo Rivera focused on "Mix & Match; Interracial Love, Sex & Marriage" during a July 1993 show. On the show was a white mother and her biracial children. Both children had the same father, a black man, yet the daughter considered herself black and the son identified himself as white. According to the sister, she had to endure racist name-calling from her own brother. He, in turn, had to defend his choice to his sister, who constantly told him he was black and not white. On the same show, however, another young brother and sister of both African-American and Italian heritage had embraced a multiethnic existence and reported no problems in their childhood or adult life.

So you see everyone really handles identity differently. The conference discussed in Chapter 3 is evidence that no two families think alike. For example, while some families embrace the term "biracial," others dislike it because they say it sounds too scientific. If you're from a black/Japanese background and consider yourself both black and Japanese, that doesn't necessarily mean that the next person you meet from the same background will feel the same way. That person may simply choose to be black or Japanese. Rather than try to change that person's views, like the sister on Geraldo's show, you'll have to respect his or her choice. After all, isn't that what you're seeking: respect for who you are? Of course it's OK to voice your opinion, but be sure to talk "with" and not talk "at" the other person. The difference? If you're talking with someone there is likely to be exchange of views. Both of you listen to each other. When you talk "at" someone, you're speaking as an authority and probably not listening to the other's views. So be sure to talk with the other person. You will probably learn that the circumstances that led to the decision about how to handle his or her racial identity were different from yours. Then again, talking with someone else about your own personal experiences may help both of you sort out even more issues. Outside of your family, this could be another support group.

Having some sort of support system is crucial for anyone, especially for teenagers, who often have low self-esteem. Parents play a major role in that support structure. Take, for example, the parents who taught their children to identify themselves as "humans." They were so adamant about their children's biracial identity that they wrote a letter to their teachers and school counselors. The letter described the family's philosophy and requested that school personnel respect their children's wish to be called "biracial" or "human" rather than be labeled "black" or "white." What kind of feelings do you have about that situation? Give it some thought.

Dealing with the kids at school is slightly different from dealing with teachers. Although we'd like to think of educators as being free of prejudice, we should not forget that they are merely human. They too are capable of exhibiting negative attitudes and of allowing their personal views to interfere with their teaching. What do you do when you encounter a teacher whose mind isn't as open as the classroom door?

Educators often go through seminars and training programs or are asked to read literature that would help them provide supportive environments for their students. But not every school district is able to provide such programs, and not every teacher will take the time to participate.

The parents who write to their children's teachers establish open lines of communication between themselves and the teachers.

Opening communication in this way is in line with some of the suggestions offered by Paula Phillips, director of Bi-Racial Families Resource Center, and Francis Wardle, Ph.D., director of the Adams County Head State and Adams County Day Care in Denver. They suggest that teachers meet with the parents of interracial children and discuss their feelings about the children's cultural and racial heritage, how the parents support that heritage at home, and how they would like to see it supported at school. People of varying cultural and racial heritages should be included in all teachers' curriculum planning. With the new emphasis on celebrating cultural diversity, many schools, especially universities, have made such teaching mandatory.

If you find that a teacher always defines the world by categories of color and physical attributes, uses stereotypes, and seems uneasy around you or your parents, you have a problem. If you feel tense about the way a teacher handles issues of race in the classroom, and you feel comfortable talking about it with that teacher, you should do so. But tell your parents first, so they can help you should problems arise.

An article in the January 1987 issue of *Young Children* deals with helping teachers relate to interracial children and their parents. Written by Francis Wardle, "Are you sensitive to interracial children's special identity needs?" offers many suggestions for teachers. It provides materials that support the parents and the children and points out how to avoid stereotyping people. Wardle is the father of a biracial daughter and has written many articles on the subject of interracial families.

Teachers can be insensitive to biracial children. For example, one teacher erroneously asked an Asian-American/white child to write some Chinese characters on the board. The child had been born and raised in New York and had never learned her father's native language. The teacher made an unfortunate assumption that caused the child great discomfort. Other prevailing ideas about Asians is that they automatically know karate, mathematics, and science. It's no surprise that such stereotyping is particularly disturbing for the children of Asian-American/white unions who are entirely American in culture.

If you don't feel comfortable confronting your teacher or administrator, and not many teens do, seek out a parent, family member, or school counselor to give you support in addressing your concerns to that teacher. Shouldn't teachers be confronted?

Sometimes legal action is necessary, or sometimes a change of teachers will solve *your* problem with that teacher. Unfortunately, it won't solve his or her problem with your racial heritage. A teacher who is insensitive, and has not examined his or her own feelings about interracial marriages or issues of race and ethnicity, cannot work effectively with interracial children and their parents. It's best to move to another class. Just remember, it is the teacher who has the problem, not you!

Some parents give their interracial children wise words to protect themselves from verbal and physical abuse. What are some of your favorite responses when someone inquires about your racial identity or calls you a name? "Oreo," "half-breed," "zebra," "nigger kid," "chocolate chip," "high yellow," "white nigger," "karate kid," "camel jockey," and "coconut," are all names teenagers say they have been called by peers or strangers on the streets. It's not easy to shrug off verbal attacks or to turn the other cheek. Your parents have no doubt urged you to live by the old saying: "Sticks and stones will break my bones but names will never hurt me." But name-calling does hurt. Just remember, those who resort to name-calling have little or no self-esteem, have little tolerance for people who are different from themselves, and want to inflict pain and show their contempt and hostility for others. People who use racial slurs don't feel bad or guilty about it, especially if they get a response from the person on the receiving end. So responding irrationally to racial slurs (which are based on irrational thinking, anyway) gives the name-caller more fuel for the fire. You can easily douse the flames by not responding, or by reacting in an unanticipated manner such as with sympathy or humor.

Author Kathlyn Gay relates numerous stories in her book *The Rainbow Effect* on how interracial and multiethnic families cope with attitudes and prejudices. One parent told the story of her white/black child who had been tormented by a classmate's constant name-calling. A visit to the principal didn't resolve the problem. The teacher did. The teacher took the biracial child's hand, and together they stood in the corner. "All those in the class who want to use ugly names and call Elliot a 'nigger' will have to call me one too," she announced. Unbeknownst to the children, their light-skinned teacher was also biracial. The name-calling stopped. But Elliot didn't let it end there. The next day, Elliot walked up to the name-caller, grabbed him around the waist, and hugged him. "What you need is some love, Zachery," Elliot said. He also told Zachery's mother that she should spend more time with her son. "He just needs to be loved so he won't be so mean," he told her.

By the same token, be sure you're not being paranoid. You don't want to live life on the defensive, waiting for someone to say something bad about you. Be yourself. Not all questions are asked out of hostility. Other people may be uncomfortable about differences, so they stare or ask questions based on fear and ignorance. Or they could just be admiring your complexion or your hair texture or the way you dress.

You have a lot of support; just look around. People who don't respect you are not important. If your paths cross, say, on a group project, deal with the person on an academic level rather than a personal one. If talking with the person doesn't help, change to another group. Keep in mind that it's the other person who has missed out on a unique chance to work with a teenager who's probably the most open-minded, confident, and mature adolescent in the classroom.

There will be missed opportunities for other teenagers

who refuse to include you in their circle of friends because of your racial identity. Many biracial adults say they encountered the most rejection in dating—not from the person they wanted to date, but from the person's parents. This author has written another book in this series, *Coping with Interracial Dating*, that suggests additional coping skills. There is no evidence that socializing, dating included, is more difficult for interracial individuals than anyone else in this society. Boy meets girl. Girl likes boy. Boom, they fall in love. Right? Again, life isn't always that simple.

Some people think that biracial couples may face rejection from both sides of their families, especially when things get romantic. For example, a teen from a black/Hispanic family may find little acceptance from either blacks or Hispanics. Other people believe that biracial people can pick and choose friends and dating partners from any cultural group. What have your experiences been? Is dating a problem for you? The world is fast turning into a society where the minority will be the majority. Predictions for that are as close as the year 2000. But as long as our society is run by humans, racism and prejudice are not likely to disappear. Can you imagine a world free of prejudice?

Ideally, we date people because we are attracted to them, we enjoy their company and personality, and we enjoy the same activities. We choose our friends the same way. But it's safe to say you should be prepared for outside pressures. For example, you may have spent your entire childhood playing with the kid next door, but if as you grow older you start finding each other attractive, to your surprise the kid's parents might be against *that* kind of relationship. It'll hurt. You'll probably feel confused about a kind of thinking that indicates it's OK to be friends but not to date across racial lines. Many parents encourage their children to date people of their own background. They expect their children to follow their lead. For a white family, a biracial teen from a white/black background may not be exactly what they pictured for their blond-haired, blue-eyed child, especially if that teen is, in their eyes, black.

Talk with your date about your racial identity and whether or not his or her family is likely to accept or reject you, and discuss how the two of you will handle any cultural differences. Communication is the key.

Knowing exactly who you are is important too, because if you are not sure of yourself, you might mistakenly accept the labels that other people put on you. Let's look at Hollywood. It's make-believe, but the people who work there are real. There are many biracial individuals in the entertainment world. Among them are actress-singer Jasmine Guy, singer Vanity, ice skating champion Tai Babilonia, former Miss America Suzette Charles, actresses Rae Dawn Chong, Rain Pryor (daughter of comedianactor Richard Pryor), Jennifer Beals, and Lisa Bonet, actor Mario Van Peebles, musicians Lenny Kravitz and Prince, and singers Mariah Carey, Neneh Cherry, SADE, Irene Cara, and Paula Abdul.

Articles in *Ebony* and *Jet* magazines raked a few of these performers over the coals for allegedly not "owning up" to their black heritage. Dr. Alvin Poussaint was quoted in the May 1990 *Jet* article as to why individuals of mixed race may not acknowledge their black side:

"Because they are biracial, they want to play down the significance of race, and in doing so they say, 'I'm not black.' But never, at least seldom, do they say, 'I'm not white.' Society identifies them as black and they resent being called black. They feel there is no advantage in being called black. They would rather say they are Greek, Italian or Hispanic, and not be identified with black . . . they see it as a disadvantage because American society has so many stigmas and they don't like the black side of themselves."

It was a very negative article, especially for those individuals accused of not owning up to who they are. Or at least to who they are in the eyes of others. What do you think? Some teens have reported incidents in which they have been accused of acting like a person of one particular race, usually the race that is the majority. Some biracial teens are belittled because they befriend members of both their races. Some teens are judged merely by the color of their skin. For example, light-skinned blacks are sometimes discriminated against by dark-skinned blacks. A biracial teen with black and white parents may be excluded from both black and white groups.

Some biracial teens of Asian or Middle Eastern ancestry are excluded from one side of their heritage because they don't speak the language, practice the customs, or wear the garb of their parent's culture.

According to many biracial individuals, the simplest coping skill is to be confident and proud of who you are.

This chapter started with a quotation from a member of Interracial Intercultural Pride (I-Pride), a support organization based in San Francisco. Bess Martinson says it's society's responsibility to recognize the fact that biracial individuals exist and that they have a place in this society. Let's see how a biracial teen relays this message to the kids and teachers at his new school.

"Class, let me have your attention. We have a new student." Mr. Erich was good at embarrassing new students. He showed this new student no mercy. "Pay attention, class. Let's show some respect!" Mr. Erich yelled above the loud talking. "This is . . . what is your name again, son?"

The denim-clad teen spoke up after clearing his throat a few times. He was obviously embarrassed but handled it well. "Brandon. Brandon Fiorentino, sir," he said in a husky voice.

"This is Brandon," Mr. Erich repeated and then hesitated. "Fiorentino? Italian, I presume."

"Yes it is," the young man replied calmly, as if being questioned about his background was no big deal. The other kids began to whisper. Veonette Diaz said, a little too loudly, that Brandon could be her "Italian stallion."

"You don't look Italian," Mr. Erich replied. The classroom was silent. It was a condition that room 302 had never experienced. Although they were all wondering themselves how this golden brown, sandy-haired teenager could be Italian, no one had ever thought about questioning him.

"That's because I left my horse's head at home, sir," Brandon replied with the same calmness he had exhibited at the first inappropriate question.

Mr. Erich's mouth dropped open. The atmosphere in the room became like the quiet before a storm. Everyone was shocked at Brandon's response. It was a response worthy of laughter, but no one dared. Someone did clear his throat loudly a few times, suggesting that he thought Mr. Erich had been put in his place. Finally, a voice came from the back of the room.

"Sit here, man." It was Glen Miles. Glen had been accepted at a naval academy. He was both intelligent and handsome. He was a little on the pompous side, constantly boasting about his future as a fighter pilot, but he was friendly. Brandon's quick wit and Glen's charm would be a definite match for Mr. Erich.

"Yes, do sit down, Mr. Fiorentino," Mr. Erich said in a biting tone. Now he was the one who was embarrassed. He mumbled "Another one" under his breath.

Brandon cleared his throat, glanced around, and proceeded to the back of the classroom. As he sauntered down the aisle he caught a few stares in his peripheral vision. He stopped at the empty desk next to Glen.

"I'm Glen. What's up?"

"Brandon." Both teens extended their hands and greeted each other with a low-five.

Mr. Erich was frantically searching his desk for something, shifting papers from one pile to the next. Everyone knew he was just trying to regroup from his confrontation with the new student. They let him continue his search in peace and locked in on Glen and Brandon's conversation.

"Thanks. What's up with him?" Brandon asked.

"He's from the old school, you know," Glen replied. "He drives a '77 Caddy, wears a toupee, and three-piece suits. Need I say more?"

Brandon smiled. Some of those overhearing Glen's description of their teacher laughed. It was right on target.

"Where are you from?" Glen asked.

"Right here in Chicago," Brandon replied as he tried to slide his tall frame into the small seat. "Man, these desks are tiny."

"You're not exactly short, Brandon," Glen reminded him. "Just how tall are you? You have to be at least six-foot."

"You taking a survey, man?" Brandon snapped back. "What's with the questions?"

Not wanting to appear as nosey as Glen, everyone

refocused their attention on Mr. Erich who appeared to be ready to continue his lecture on his favorite subject—himself.

"OK, class," Mr. Erich began. "As I was saying, I became interested in social studies from my first visit to an Indian reservation in high school. The government has done so much for those people. Our government is one of the . . ."

"Hey, I'm sorry, man," Glen whispered to Brandon as the teacher spoke about the U.S. Constitution. "I didn't mean to give you the third degree."

"No problem, man," Brandon whispered back. They gave each other another low-five. "It's tough being the new kid on the block, you know. I come from 85th and South Morgan. Know it?"

"That's kind of a rough neighborhood," Glen answered. "One of my cousins is heavy into gang-banging there. Or at least he used to be. Stupid."

"Iced?"

"Six feet under."

"Well, my mother wants me to remain six feet on top; that's why we moved to Hyde Park. You know, single parent, absent father. I can't be in all the statistics," Brandon said.

"Gang-bangers try to recruit you?" Glen asked.

"Not hardly, man. Look at this face," Brandon whispered back, turning one cheek toward Glen but keeping one eye on the teacher. "I couldn't be down with anything—even if I wanted to. I don't quite look like the other brothers in the hood, now do I?"

Glen suddenly felt slightly uncomfortable. The idea of the color of Brandon's skin keeping him out of something so negative as a street gang was almost too much to swallow. Prejudiced gang-bangers? Now, there's a new one, he thought to himself. He still couldn't find a come-back for Brandon. It was OK because Brandon had more to say.

"My mom is Italian, and she says my dad was black," Brandon continued to whisper, this time ignoring the teacher and facing Glen completely. "Together, you get me—not dark enough to be black, not light enough to be Italian. Caused too much trouble in the hood for the other fellas to deal with. Always on my back about my color. I guess I need my own gang, you know what I mean?"

Glen didn't know, because both his parents were white and so was he. But a few of his other friends were biracial. He detected in Brandon's green eyes a sense that his biracial identity was an issue he was trying to cope with. He could only ask a question. "So what do you consider yourself, black or Italian?"

"Since it's just me and Moms, I'm her son. I'm a Fiorentino. But . . ." Brandon didn't get to finish. Mr. Erich ended the conversation.

"Excuse me, gentlemen!" he reproved. "I am trying to conduct a class here. I don't know where it is you come from, Mr. Fiorentino, but here on this side of town we're in school to learn. We don't need your kind disrupting the educational process here."

Your kind? Everyone wanted clarification now. Exactly what was the teacher referring to? Was it the fact that Brandon was from a rough neighborhood? But how would Mr. Erich know that? Or was it that Brandon was obviously biracial? The eyes and heads in the classroom quickly shifted between Mr. Erich and Brandon. It was as if they were watching a tennis match. It was Brandon's turn.

"I'm sorry, Mr. Erich, I was asking Brandon a question," Glen spoke up. But the teacher wouldn't let it rest. It appeared that he had it in for Brandon.

"I was addressing Mr. Fiorentinnnooo," Mr. Erich spoke firmly. Things had become very nasty.

Here was a terrible situation brewing. If you were Brandon, how would you have handled it? Mr. Erich's comments about "this side of town" and "your kind" were totally out of line. So was the way he lingered on the vowel sounds of the Italian surname. Brandon was a new kid who was talking while the teacher was lecturing. He had to own up to that. Brandon also had to be careful how he responded because Mr. Erich was an adult. Adults demand respect even when they aren't showing much themselves. A teenager may have to play the adult in these situations. Let's see how Brandon handled himself.

Everyone waited for Brandon's response with intense anticipation. They all wanted Brandon to really give Mr. Erich a tongue-lashing that would put him in his place.

Mr. Erich was a teacher with outmoded ways of thinking. He had never adjusted to the school's or the community's integrated population. Even some teachers at the school disliked him. Yet, he was still teaching, still sprinkling his lectures with derogatory comments about any race or religion that wasn't like his: white Anglo-Saxon Protestant.

The confrontation never came. The lunch bell sounded. Class was over. Usually everyone was out the door and munching on Doritos before the last ring. Today, no one moved from their seats; everyone wanted to see what would happen.

"Excuse me, Mr. Erich," a soft voice came from the front of the room. It was Vanessa Perez. Vanessa, like Brandon, was biracial. Her mother was white, her father was Puerto Rican. She was the most articulate of her classmates, destined to be in public office. "I don't think you're being fair to Brandon. In fact, I don't think you've been fair to any of the kids in this school who aren't like you. With all due respect, I think you're a racist and shouldn't be teaching here or any other place, for that matter."

Everyone in the classroom started clapping. "You tell him, girlfriend!" and "It's about time someone told him off!" were just some of the comments buzzing over the applause.

"And what do you mean by that, Ms. Perez!" Mr. Erich shouted.

"She means, you should realize that you're prejudiced!" Sue Schneider nearly screamed. "It's people like you who make me embarrassed to be white."

"Well, I've never . . .!" Mr. Erich huffed.

"And that's part of your problem," interjected Darin Wheat, who at age sixteen was already the parent of an interracial child. "You've never taken the time to realize that people are people. When are you so-called grown-ups going to learn that? What difference does color make? We're all going to live, and we're all going to die."

"What's going to die, Mr. Wheat, is the purity of all races," Mr. Erich responded. "What we'll soon have here is a planet of mutts."

Everyone began to grumble about that comment.

"The United States has denied the reality of racial mixing as fervently as it has upheld the myth of the melting pot, Mr. Erich," Vanessa said calmly. It was hard to believe she was only sixteen. "People of different races and cultural backgrounds can and do achieve racial harmony. They fall in love, marry, and produce us— mutts, as you say. But we have just as much right to be here as you or anyone else. Racial purity is the fantasy of cavemen. We are not mutts, we are humans, and we're not going away. So get used to it. With all due respect, I mean."

Again thunderous applause filled the room. Brandon was the only one not clapping. He was in shock. The second lunch bell rang, and this time everyone started filing out of the room, leaving an embattled Mr. Erich standing at his desk with his mouth hanging open.

Glen stood up, and turned to see Brandon still sitting.

"Welcome to Hyde Park, man," Glen said, lifting his hand in the air for a high-five.

Brandon stood and gave Glen his high-five. "Yeah, I'm going to like it here," he said. "Who was that girl?"

"That girl was *my* girl!" Glen responded. "So don't even try it, Mr. Italian Stallion."

Brandon, who towered over Glen, looked down at his new friend and with a boyish grin said, "Hey, it's Mr. *black*-Italian Stallion."

Did you expect Brandon's new classmates to come to his defense the way they did? Neither did he. Biracial people often find support and less prejudice in integrated communities and schools. Teenagers today are a lot wiser than those of yesterday. You may find that your peers are less tolerant of the racism that is destroying our society the way environmental hazards are eating away at the ozone layer. If we don't make changes fast, we'll lose them both.

CHAPTER 5

Celebrating Diversity

Discriminate: to make a difference in treatment or favor on a basis other than individual merit. One word. Four syllables. Yet, a concept that has had a devastating effect on the world. It's a behavior no one is born with; it has to be learned. Read carefully how one child learns what discrimination is:

A first-grade teacher before letting her class out for recess informed them of a small task they would have to do in order to receive their snacks. "Now when you come back in, boys and girls, you have to be able to tell me what you did at recess and be able to spell all the words," the teacher said. "If you can do that, I'll give you your milk and cookies."

The first child to come in from recess was Johnny. He was the spitting image of Opie on the old "Andy Griffith" show. "Little Johnny," said the teacher, "what did you do at recess?"

"I played in the sandbox with Lisa. It was fun."

"Good, Johnny. If you can spell 'sand' you can have your milk and cookies."

"S-A-N-D," the child said. He sat down and ate his snack.

Next to come in was a blond-haired girl in pigtails.

"Lisa," said the teacher. "What did you do at recess?"

"I played in the sandbox with Johnny. It was a lot of fun."

"Good, Lisa. If you can spell 'box' you can have your milk and cookies."

"B-O-X," the child said and joined Johnny.

Next to come in was Leroy, a black child. Leroy slowly walked in with his head down. It appeared he had been crying.

"Why, what's the matter, Leroy?" the teacher asked.

"They wouldn't let me play in the sandbox. They told me to get out," he sulked.

"Why, Leroy," the teacher replied, "that's racial discrimination. If you can spell 'discrimination,' you can have YOUR milk and cookies."

This was an actual joke told to a black woman by a white coworker. Was it funny? Of course, it wasn't funny, but it illustrated very powerfully how children learn about discrimination at a very early age. The operative word here is "learn." Racial discrimination or any other form of hatred is learned in the comfort of home right along with the ABCs and 1-2-3s. Children's minds are like sponges: They absorb what they hear and see daily. If their parents smoke, chances are they will too. If their parents read every night, chances are they will too. If their parents refer to people of racial/ethnic backgrounds different from their own with stereotypes and racial slurs, chances are their children will adopt those same negative views.

You're smart enough to know that racist attitudes are held by people of color as well as nonminority people. Prejudice lies even within a race.

Hatred, discrimination, prejudice, and racism are nothing new to this society.

> Once riding in old Baltimore,
> Heart-filled, head-filled with glee,
> I saw a Baltimorean
> Keep looking straight at me.
>
> Now I was eight and very small,
> And he was no whit bigger,
> And so I smiled, but he poked out
> His tongue, and called me a "Nigger."
>
> I saw the whole Baltimore
> From May until December,
> Of all things that happened there
> That's all that I remember.

The American/poet Countee Cullen forged those words from an incident in his childhood. It's one of many pieces in *I Am the Darker Brother: An Anthology of Modern Poems by Negro Americans*. By the age of six, most African-American children learn a lesson similar to the one Cullen had that day in Baltimore: that blackness more often evokes contempt, fear, and ridicule than it does positive images from mainstream America. Are race relations in this society getting better? Let's see . . .

At the University of Georgia, a student from Singapore had eggs thrown through his dormitory window. A Confederate flag was planted outside the window along with a note containing anti-Asian slogans . . . In California, a Torrey Pines State Reserve ranger discovered several fraternity members from the University of San Diego participating in a cross-burning ritual. The group denied the incident was racially motivated, apologized, and later discontinued the initiation rite . . . In Arizona, fraternity members from the University of Arizona campus in Tucson wouldn't admit four black male students to their party. A fight broke out, and a police officer was killed . . . Three blacks were attacked for being in the Howard Beach area of Queens, New York. One was struck and killed by a car as he fled across a highway . . . In Boston, Massachusetts, a fake employment form was circulated through an employee lounge at an emergency medical services department, asking blacks to fill in the names of their "motha" and "fatha" and asking Hispanics to select their favorite foods from a list of "beans, beans and tortillas, tortillas and beans, tortillas" . . . A black teenager was killed by a mob in the Bensonhurst section of Brooklyn, New York, when residents thought he was dating a white girl . . . In California, a black motorist was brutally beaten by four white police officers after a high-speed chase. The officers were acquitted, sparking the worst riots in Los Angeles's history . . . In Florida, a black tourist was robbed, tortured, and set afire by white thugs, who were eventually convicted of all the charges against them . . . And in the Middle East, the Israelies and the Palestinians have been living under constant, deadly violent conditions . . . And Nanjing, China, experienced outbreaks of racial violence because African students were dating Chinese women.

All these events happened not in the 1960s, but in the late '80s and early '90s. Incidents such as these are evidence that the growth of racial and ethnic tensions is a trend of the '90s. The incidents may vary from city to city, state to state, country to country, and they may involve people of different races, cultures, religious beliefs, and sexual preferences. They all have one thing in common however: prejudice, discrimination, and hate.

Such outbreaks of racial tension and violence are scary. Why are we not more accepting of people who are different from us? Why are we not celebrating the diversity? Why? Because most people are not educating themselves. Prejudice forms out of fear and ignorance of the unknown. Education cures ignorance. By educating ourselves and gaining knowledge about individuals from other racial/ ethnic backgrounds, we become more sensitive to cultural and ethnic differences, and we eliminate the unknown, the ignorance, and hopefully the prejudice.

Genetically, humans are all the same. Race is a sociological term.

On the positive side, many people are trying to do something to ease racial tensions and bring people together, to celebrate the diversity. High schools in the Irvine Unified School District in California started interethnic relations programs in 1987 to help their diverse student populations get along with each other. A Phoenix high school superintendent reports that his school district has implemented a multicultural curriculum for its 20,000 students. New to Arizona, he said that race relations among the teenagers in his integrated district were considerably better than they were in New York. His own daughter, who is white, is a member of her school's Asian club. Why? Many of her friends are Asian, and they invited her to join to learn more about them and their culture. She did.

Clubs have been very effective in helping students celebrate diversity and fight racism. Just as in crime-ridden neighborhoods where many Block Watch programs are forming to take back the streets from gangs, students on high school and college campuses are fighting back against racism. You may have heard of the group Minorities Against Discrimination (M.A.D.).

Some college campuses around the country are adding cultural/ethnic awareness courses as electives, and others are making them mandatory. In these settings, students can learn about each other's history and background. They can have questions answered, breaking down stereotypes. Others campuses have established strong antihate and antiharassment policies that prohibit students and teachers from interfering with students' rights to peaceful enjoyment of the campus or the dorm. Verbal and physical attacks on people based on their race, color, religion, national origin, or sexual preference are against the rules and punishable. Although many of these rules are being challenged in the courts as violations of freedom of speech guaranteed by the United States Constitution, school administrators say such policies are necessary to create an environment where all races and cultures are respected. They're trying to keep the peace, not infringe on anyone's rights.

To further help minorities and foreign students become assimilated, school officials have created special on-campus centers, rooms, and even dorms where these students can meet other students of the same background. Although the centers are open to all students, nonminority students claim that these arrangements just create more racial tension and further separate everyone into categories. What if the nonminority visited the centers more often and established some crosscultural friendships? It would probably help change their attitudes.

Even small things help. Crayola Crayons makes crayons of "multicultural" colors described this way: "Multicultural Color assortment contains six skin tone colors of the world which can be blended with black and white to create a wide variety of skin tones. By varying pressure while crayoning, deeper or lighter tones can be achieved to expand the color range in this culturally inclusive assortment." Adhesive bandages, Multiskins, are now available in dark, medium, and light brown shades to match darker skin tones much better than the traditional pink strips. Many department stores and grocery stores across the country are adding ethnic sections, exhibiting sensitivity to ethnic/racial groups while filling some of their special needs.

It's no secret that America is changing. The two fastest-growing groups are the Asians and Hispanics. Blacks are no longer the majority among minorities. Population statistics indicate that blacks, Hispanics, Native Americans, and Asians will account for more than fifty percent of the population in the United States by the year 2000. Some areas such as Los Angeles, New York, Chicago, Dallas, and San Antonio have already reached that point.

According to demographers, the white population is declining. As reported in *U.S. News & World Report*, there were forty-five million white children under the age of eighteen in 1990. In the year 2000, the prediction is forty-three million, and in the year 2010, thirty-eight million. With society becoming more multiethnic, interracial dating and marriages seem almost inevitable. An emerging population of multiethnic children is therefore also inevitable.

One thing that most people probably hate the most is change. But hate it or not, it's a fact of life. Learning how to interact effectively with these other groups will bring about good changes. Is everyone willing to do that?

You may be surprised to learn that even minorities are prejudiced against other minorities. For example, a 1986 poll taken in Orange County, California, revealed that whites think Hispanics are lazy and that Vietnamese people will stop at nothing to get ahead. Hispanics and Vietnamese think that whites are uninterested in their families and don't keep up their homes well. Vietnamese think Hispanics place too much importance on religion.

Ask some people you know to finish this sentence, "All blacks are . . ." Use any race or culture. You'll be surprised to find that it's commonly believed that all Chinese know kung fu, all Colombians deal drugs, all blacks have rhythm, all Irish people are drunks, all Mexicans drive low-riders, all Native Americans live on reservations, and all Asians are workaholics. Intraracism exists as well— people stereotyping their own race. For example, light-skinned blacks often receive hostile reactions from darker skinned blacks.

Outside of family life, television, newspapers, and movies do an excellent job of stereotyping people. They continue to perpetuate the stereotypes when stories about gang violence depict only black or Hispanic members, when stories about organized crime show only Italians, when white-collar crime is done by the white man, and stories about the welfare system depict only black women. In the early 1980s, an Arizona State University researcher found that things were improving where stereotypes were concerned. Having been conducting the study since the 1960s, for the first time he found both negative and positive images of various racial and ethnic groups. For example, blacks were viewed as "intelligent" and "sportsmanlike," which he considered positives. But they were also viewed as "sly," "loud," and "arrogant." There were also more positive and negative stereotypes of Hispanics, Native Americans, Jewish people, and Asians.

What is causing these racial tensions? Researchers say that much of it on college and high school campuses has to do with competition for jobs and "making it" in the real world. A white student may view an Asian student as someone who's going to get better grades and throw off the grading curve, causing the white student's grades to be lower. You've seen this at the bottom of many job listings in the classified section of newspapers: Equal Opportunity Employer. You've no doubt heard of affirmative action programs. These types of programs are designed to bring educational and career opportunities to minorities and women who simply didn't have the chances before. Many nonminority people object to the programs because they wrongly believe that special treatment is being given to minorities, causing them to lose out on jobs and promotions.

There is some paranoia on both sides. Interracial families and people involved in interracial relationships should not always think they're the center of attention, although the more visually apparent the differences are, the more they will stand out. The more they stand out, the more people will take notice. We look at Ferraris speeding down the street, don't we? Our nation is obsessed with color and categorizing people. From the day you were born, you were placed in a category: white, boy; black, girl; Chinese, girl; Indian, boy; and so on. If your parents didn't do it, the hospital personnel did. Today, with the birth of biracial children, the classification system is becoming very confused. Parents of biracial children are refusing to classify a child by one race only when it is the product of two.

Harvard University in 1992–93 placed a "multiethnic" category on its admission application. Other schools across the country are slowly following suit. Finally some good things are beginning to take root.

But realize that ethnic and racial tensions, prejudice

and discrimination are not erased by the stroke of a pen. Education is the key to improving human relationships.

Your parents' interracial dating said more than, "Hey, look at us; we're in love." It said, "Hey, two people of different races can not only get along but love each other, and no one has to get hurt." Racial harmony is a sound yet to be heard around the world.

Like it or not, you're part of the educational process. You may just want to fade into the woodwork hoping everyone will just "leave you alone" and "mind their own business," but chances are you won't go unnoticed. Don't you want to stand up and be counted?

Gail Mathabane, coauthor of *Love in Black and White* and mother of two biracial children, writes in the July 1992 issue of *American Baby*, "The beauty of interracial children is their complete lack of prejudice. They move fluidly between the white and black worlds, unaware of the tension between them. My main hope for my children is that Americans adhere to the dream of an integrated society. Only in an integrated society will biracial children be fully appreciated for what they are: living proof that the races do not have to hate one another."

It should be remembered that apart from the Native Americans, all us are descended from people who came from somewhere else.

AFRICA: At the time of George Washington's inauguration in 1789, one fifth of the population was black. African-Americans make up twelve percent of Americans in the 1990s but remain the country's largest ethnic minority.

BRITISH ISLES: The English, Welsh, Scottish, and Irish peoples began migration early, formed the basis of the American-European culture, and gave it a language.

FRANCE: French commercial and imperial penetration of North America paralleled that of the English. They were defeated in the French and Indian War by the English and gave up their last American territories with the Louisiana Purchase. Many French-speaking people remained here.

GERMANY AND AUSTRIA: From the 1600s onward there was steady immigration. By 1990, at least one quarter of Americans identified themselves as being at least part German.

EASTERN EUROPE: Russian, Polish, Ukrainian, Czechoslovakian, Romanian, Bulgarian, Hungarian, Yugoslavian, Estonian, and Latvian peoples, among them many Jews, came in waves.

DENMARK, NORWAY, AND SWEDEN: From 1851 on, these peoples settled predominantly in the Middle West.

INDIA, PAKISTAN, AND BANGLADESH: This migration began in 1965.

MEXICO AND LATIN AMERICA: No other ethnic or national group is known by more labels than this group of immigrants.

THE CARIBBEAN: Some of our earliest immigrants have been from Cuba and Jamaica. Since 1965, many more have begun to come.

GREECE: A large group of Americans have emigrated from Greece and the Greek Islands.

ITALY: These are a diverse groups of immigrants, mainly from southern Italy or Sicily; they have lately been joined by northern Italians.

CHINA: Chinese were among the earliest groups to immigrate, many coming under contract to build the railroads.

THE MIDDLE EAST: These immigrants are very diverse and include many nationalities. They are linked by the Arabic language.

Let's end this chapter with a true celebration of diversity. *TIME* magazine's Fall 1993 issue is all about the new face of America. One article, "The Art of Diversity," discusses Cuban-American singing star Gloria Estefan appearing on MTV Latino; the 1993 release of the movie *The Joy Luck Club*, based on a popular novel by Chinese-American author Amy Tan; Garth Fagan, a Jamaican-American choreographer who directs the modern-dance show "Griot New York"; Nobel Prize-winning poet and St. Lucia-born Derek Walcott; and a tour of Asian-American visual artists who emigrated from Vietnam, Thailand, and elsewhere in Asia. One of them is Japanese-born painter Masami Teraoka. The article points out that the Los Angeles rap trio Cypress Hill includes an Italian-American, a Cuban-American, and a member who is of Cuban and Mexican descent.

The article also talks about the Los Angeles-based firm Thread for Life (also known as Cross Colours), which sells hip-hop fashions inspired by urban youth and African designers.

What will leave the biggest impression on the millions of Americans who read this issue is the cover picture: a woman created by a computer process called morphing. She was selected as a symbol of the future—the multiethnic face of America. She doesn't really exist. A combination of the racial and ethnic features of the women used to produce the chart, the woman on the cover is: 15 percent Anglo-Saxon, 17.5 percent Middle Eastern, 17.5 percent African, 7.5 percent Asian, 35 percent Southern European, and 7.5 percent Hispanic. The creator of the image? Kin Wah Lam.

CHAPTER 6

Check the Box

Marked "Other"

T he third-graders in Miss Overton's class had a guest speaker one day: a private investigator who discussed fingerprinting and actually fingerprinted all of the children. Before their prints were taken, the students were asked to complete an official "applicant" card to experience the real effect of being fingerprinted. Miss Overton helped the youngsters complete the card by going over each section step-by-step.

When it came time to fill in the box for racial identity, she instructed the children as follows: "If you're African-American, put 'B' for black; if you're of European descent, put 'W' for white; if you're Hispanic-American, put 'H' in the box; if you're Asian-American, put an 'A' there; and if you're Native American, put an 'I' for Indian. Did everyone get that?"

One of the small tykes spoke up. "What if you're mixed? Do you put an 'M' for mixed?"

Miss Overton was caught off guard. "No, an 'M' would be taken as Mexican."

"What do I put? I'm Mexican and black, so do I put 'MB'?"

Before the teacher could answer, another student spoke up.

"Yeah, what do we put? I'm mixed Mexican and black and so is Alisha, and Chris, and Jessica."

Yet another. "Teacher, I'm mixed white and Mexican."

And finally another student. "I'm white and black. I put 'WB'; is that OK?"

These third-graders have really simplified a process that adults have managed to make so complex: the U.S. Census. Every ten years, the United States sets out to find out how many people are living in this country. The last one was taken in 1990. Surveys are sent out to every household in America. Census takers even hit the streets to count the homeless. One of the things asked on this survey is your race and the race of family members. Current categories are unquestionably inadequate. Multiple choice answers include white, black, American Indian, Eskimo, Aleut, and nine varieties of Asian or Pacific Islanders. Until 1980, the census didn't even have a "Hispanic" category. Operators at a toll-free 800 number advise multiracial people who inquire to choose whichever one race they most identify with. What about the other race—or races—that are equally a part of your identity?

Most parents feel that checking the box marked "other" is not acceptable; that it's psychologically damaging to force somebody to choose one identity when physiologically and biologically they are more than one.

There are definite problems with the current classifying and categorization of people. Inaccurate figures are reported. For example, between 1970 and 1980, the number of interracial married couples more than doubled, according to U.S. census figures. By 1990, the census counted 211,000 interracial married couples. However, the census undercounts interracial couples because it tallies only black/white couples and keeps no figures at all on the multiracial children.

Professors at major universities have been quoted in numerous articles pinpointing the problem. "The Census Bureau has gone through years of denial, insisting that there is such a thing as a pure race," one said. Another professor undertook his own count by combing through California's marriage-license and other records and conducting surveys and interviews. What he found was that more than thirty-five percent of Asians in California marry interracially, as well as seventy percent of U.S.-born Asians between ages twenty-five and forty, and eighteen percent of African-Americans. Using these figures as a basis, the professor estimates that at least ten percent of marriages taking place nationally are mixed-race marriages. The Census figures report a mere one half of one percent! Furthermore, if these marriages produce the average 2.2 children, a multiracial society is inevitable.

To correct the problem, many multicultural organizations, like the San Franciso-based Association of Multi-Ethnic Americans (AMEA) and Project RACE (Reclassify All Children Equally) of Atlanta, are pushing for the inclusion of a "mixed-race" category in the official Census by the year 2000. Founded in 1988 as a confederation of local multiethnic and interracial groups, the AMEA encourages individuals of mixed race to claim their whole identities: to stand up and be counted for who they are. It also makes society aware of the issues. Project RACE was formed in 1991 with an objective to mandate a multiracial category on all forms requiring racial data. As a result of their efforts, school districts in the Atlanta area, Cincinnati, Ohio and DeKalb County, Georgia added a multiracial category for all students. Addresses for these and others are given in the Help List on p. 115.

You're probably very excited about these new categories, saying to yourself, "Yes, I'll finally have a box to check." Do you think everyone shares your excitement? If you read about this issue you will find that many African-American organizations are against the proposal, saying it would dilute political unity among black people. They fear that with the addition of a new racial category, mixed-race persons who are black and white will abandon the black race, leaving it politically and economically weaker.

What is the solution? Not having a biracial or multiracial category denies biracial individuals recognition and representation. Having one creates some tension. What about getting rid of racial categories altogether? Is knowing that there are so many Japanese-Americans or so many blacks or so many Native Americans really that important?

Racial categories aren't just used for number crunching. They are used for things like affirmative action, a government program designed to make sure underrepresented groups, such as minorities, are given job opportunities. But there are controversies surrounding this program as well. What do you think? What do your parents think? Talk to them about it. If you feel strongly about the creation of a new racial category, you may want to join the battle. Contact AMEA or Project RACE if you do.

In the meantime, meet Leanderson and Omar. They are brothers, identical twins. Their father is Iranian, and their mother is Native American and white. They are juniors in a public school located in a predominantly white area in a small Midwestern town. Today is College Day, when the entire junior class spends the day traveling from classroom to classroom learning about various universities.

"What's on your schedule?" Don asked his best buddy, Leanderson.

Looking at his list, Leanderson read the list of college representatives he was supposed to see first. "Let's see," he mumbled, "first there's Yale, then Harvard, then Princeton."

"Yeah, right!" Don shot back at him. "Get serious."

Leanderson tried not to laugh, but even he couldn't keep a straight face telling this fib. It wasn't that he was dumb; he just didn't apply himself to his studies with the same determination and focus he applied to Ming, his girlfriend. Chances are, if he had gone to the library on all the nights he *said* he was going, he could have made the list for the Ivy-League schools he joked about.

"Now, you know what's up. I could be hobnobbing with the rich and famous, having champagne dreams and caviar wishes, if I wanted to, wearing argyles with my Birkenstocks," Leanderson joked. "But I can't live without my 501 Blues and my Nikes, so I'd rather spend my college career with my best buddy."

"No, you'd rather spend your boring and brainless self with your honey," Don teased him back. "Now, what's on the list?"

Leanderson stop laughing long enough to recite his four college picks. "Michigan, Purdue, North Carolina, and UCLA!"

"I can't believe UCLA came out here," Don said excitedly. "We lucked out."

"Cool," Leanderson replied. "Let's do it."

Don and Leanderson had been best friends since junior high school. Don grew up in a Wisconsin farm town where folks didn't have to lock their houses and everyone knew everyone else. It was sixty miles from any major city. A long way from the reality of the great cities. Don wanted to expand his horizons, so he moved in with his grandmother. He met Leanderson on the first day at his new school. He'll never forget that day.

Don and Leanderson were selected to work together on a class project. They were instructed to interview each other and write two-page biographies about each other. As they sat in the library going through the list of questions, which ranged from "Where were you born?" to "What are your career plans?" another male student accidentally bumped into Don's chair. This caused Don's pencil to run off the page. He let out an obscenity.

"I hate those Indians," Don said, as he erased his mistake. "They were all over the town I came from. I'm surprised he doesn't smell like whiskey like all the rest of them . . . OK, next question. What race are you?" Before Leanderson could answer or even make a comment on Don's attack on Indians, Don continued. "I know this one." He wrote in the word "white" because Leanderson did appear to be white.

"Hold up, man," Leanderson said, grabbing Don's pencil. "My name mother is half Navajo, so I guess that makes me an Indian too, now doesn't it?"

"Yeah, sure, you're an Indian," Don replied with obvious disbelief. He reached to take his pencil back, but the look on Leanderson's face was serious. When Leanderson broke Don's pencil in half and threw it on the floor, Don knew he had made a big mistake.

"You're serious, aren't you?"

"Do I look serious?" Leanderson replied sharply.

"Well, I don't mean you . . . I mean . . . open mouth, insert foot," Don said, admitting he'd said the wrong thing. "I didn't know."

"And that justifies your hatred toward my people, or any other race for that matter?" Leanderson responded. He was quite calm. As a biracial teen, he had learned to handle the many Dons in the world. He was proud of his racial heritage. He and his brother Omar had grown up having their racial identity questioned. They had been thought to be Tongans, Kenyans, Cubans, and even Hawaiians. Rarely did people guess the mix.

"No, it doesn't," Don said shamefaced. "I'm really sorry."

"Don't feel sorry for me," Leanderson replied. "Feel sorry for yourself. You're the one with the problem."

There was a brief moment of silence. Until the racial slur came out of his mouth, Don had seemed like a decent guy. Leanderson decided he was worth trying to educate. "Look man, you're just ignorant," Leanderson continued. "I don't deny my biracial roots: I am part Iranian, part Native-American, and part white."

Don looked even more surprised.

"Wouldn't have guessed it, huh?" Leanderson teased. "You know why I don't have to deny my roots? Because everyone does it for me. So they feel better about being friends with me, I guess. The Iranians say, 'We'll ignore his white and Indian sides,'" he continued. "And the whites say, 'We'll tune out his Iranian side.' Native Americans just tune me out altogether most of the time."

"So how do you deal with it?" Don asked.

"How do you deal with being white?" Leanderson quickly shot back. "Race is not a factor in what type of person I am. I'm me. I've never felt, 'I wish I weren't half and half' or felt mad at my parents. I don't have any problems with society; society has an issue with me because I can't be placed into a neat box. I won't be placed in a box until they make one just for me—all of me. Get it?"

"Yeah, I get it," Don said. And he did get it. "Thanks for educating me instead of punching my lights out. I hope we can still be friends. I could sure use one."

"How about two?" Leanderson said, noticing his brother walking toward them.

"What do you mean?" Don asked, following Leanderson's eyes. "Whoa! There are two of you . . . I mean . . . you're twins. Cool."

"Yeah, but I was born one minute earlier," Omar said, pulling up a chair next to his brother.

"But I got the looks," Leanderson bellowed.

Don smiled at his new friends.

Omar got the last word. "But I got the brains," he said. It was true. Although they were twins, Omar was a senior on his way to Stanford, then on to medical school.

"This is Donny Price," Leanderson quickly introduced his new friend so he wouldn't have to listen to his brother talk about how smart he was.

"Don," Don said, extending his hand for a handshake. Omar obliged.

"You know, Don, the Indians started the handshake," Leanderson said. "It was a gesture to show the white man that the Indian came in peace and didn't have any weapons in his hand. Of course, he was making sure the white man didn't have any weapons either."

They all laughed, and from then on Don and Leanderson were best pals.

Have you ever been in Leanderson's situation? Has anyone ever jumped to conclusions about your heritage? Has anyone ever discounted any part of your background? It takes a really confident person to hold back one's emotions and deal with the situation when faced with discrimination or prejudice. An important part of what Leanderson said was that he was proud of who he was. He also said that he couldn't be placed in a neat box. He was the sum of many parts. He was very sure of his identity.

Biracial teens in the 1990s are having quite different experiences from those in the 1970s. Decades ago, biracial teens were few and far between. Biracial adults say they had to choose one race or another, denying either their mother or father. Usually, they weren't accepted fully as members of either race. Today's young biracial people are better able to deal with their identity because society is finally beginning to take notice, thanks to the many groups that have formed. But society continues trying to force multiracial individuals into boxes that are meant for single-race people.

Let's go back to Leanderson and Don as they attend Career Day.

"Which one should we go to first?" Leanderson asked, knowing full well that they were to follow the schedule given to them by the school counselor.

"Need you ask?" Don said. He pointed to room A24 where a sign outside the door read: University of California at Los Angeles.

"We're there!" The classroom was jam-packed. It appeared everyone wanted to hear about UCLA.

"Front row?" Don asked Leanderson. Actually, the two front seats were their only choice. Just as they sat down, the UCLA representative walked into the room.

"I'm glad so many of you turned out today," the well-dressed man said. "I know you all were expecting me to show up in colorful shorts down to my knees, wearing sunglasses and a tan, and singing a Beach Boys song." They all laughed.

"Well, if you think UCLA is all about surf and sun," he continued, "I'm about to disappoint you." They all moaned. "My name is Mr. Kruger, yes, as in Freddie." They all laughed. This man was good.

"I'm here to talk to you about the University of California at Los Angeles," he continued. "Our students do more than hang ten. In fact, it's probably easier to surf during a hurricane than get into UCLA. Good education doesn't come easy or cheap. But we have great scholarships available."

Mr. Kruger talked for about twenty-five minutes as everyone gave him undivided attention. After his talk, he passed out admissions and scholarship applications.

"Can I get a minority scholarship application?" Leanderson asked Mr. Kruger when the session was over. The man gave him a puzzled look as he handed over the application.

"My school records say I'm white because there wasn't a box to check for what I really am, and my parents refused to check just one box," Leanderson explained. "I guess over the years someone in the office made the decision that I'm white. Really, I'm part Native American, part Iranian, and part white. So that qualifies me to apply for a minority scholarship, right?"

Mr. Kruger smiled. "Yes, it does," he said. "And you'll be happy to know that there is a 'multiracial' box for you to check on all of our applications."

Leanderson smiled. "But if your school records say 'white,' you're going to have a problem," Mr. Kruger warned. "You may want to get your permanent records changed. What does your birth certificate say?"

Leanderson thought. "I think it says white, too," he said. "I remember my mother saying that the nurse checked boxes for me and my brother when my mother wouldn't. Actually, I'm a twin. My birth certificate says white; my brother's says Indian/white."

"You have quite a dilemma, young man," Mr. Kruger replied. "Unfortunately, if you don't get it cleared up now, you could face a few obstacles down the road. Have you ever heard of the Association for MultiEthnic Americans? This organization is working to get a multi-ethnic category on the Census for the year 2000.

"Here's my card," he continued. "Call me for the number. They are a very effective organization and can probably give you good advice on this matter. Good luck."

Good luck? Leanderson stood devastated with the card in his hand. He had never thought of the consequences that could occur because of his being classified incorrectly. He was angry—at society.

"What's up?" Don interrupted his thoughts. "Kruger is cool, and UCLA looks great. Did you get your application? Yo, Leanderson. Do you hear me?"

Leanderson snapped out of his trance. "You know, this society is really rotten sometimes," he said. "Biracial kids are left out. My Korean-American girlfriend's parents don't like me because to them I'm Iranian, yet tomorrow someone else will hate me because I'm white or Indian. The next time, I'm checking every box on the form!"

Don just stood there as Leanderson raged. "What's up with you?" Don finally asked. "Calm down. Let's go out in the hallway." He literally had to push Leanderson out of the classroom. Leanderson calmed down long enough to tell Don of his dilemma.

"That's rough," Don replied. "What are you going to do?"

"I'm going to call the Association of MultiEthnic Americans and join the war . . . and I have one battle to fight right now."

Leanderson turned and marched toward the student-records office.

"War? Battle? What fight?" Don called out to Leanderson, who was obviously on a mission. "Where are you going? I'm coming too. We're buddies. I'm in this war too."

A "multiracial" box would solve a lot of society's racial questions—at least on paper.

CHAPTER 7

Are You Guys

Related?

I nterracial families are not just families whose children are biracial or biethnic. A transracial adoption occurs when couples adopt children whose race is different from their own. For example, a white couple who adopt an Asian child have adopted transracially. Parents who adopt transracially cannot ignore the fact that they become an interracial multiethnic family and a minority family, subject to criticism, odd remarks, and prejudice from people of all races. Parents are likely to hear, "Where did you get her from?" or "Are you a foster parent?" The child is likely to hear comments like, "Is that your real mother?" or "Are you guys related?"

This chapter takes a brief look at transracial adoption. Although families that adopt children of different races do not face exactly the same issues as interracial families, some isues are the same for both groups of children— biracial and transracially adopted. A child involved in a transracial adoption has two issues to face: adoption, and being a member of a multiracial family. Fortunately, psychological studies have found that transracially adopted children appear to handle the identity issues all adopted children face better than most. Why? Researchers theorize that these children cannot pretend to be like everyone else.

Like biracial children, most transracially adopted teens say growing up in multiracial families has helped them to get along well with people of different races. They feel comfortable in a variety of social settings. The benefits of being part of a multiracial family spill over to all the children in the family.

There are some coping skills necessary for multiracial families. Experts say parents need to deal first with their own race issues, then help their children identify with the totality of their backgrounds. Experts advise parents to join support organizations, live in racially mixed neighborhoods, send their children to integrated schools and cultivate friends of the same race as their children. Does this sound familiar? It should. This is similar to the advice offered in early chapters to parents of biracial children. If you're a transracial adoptee, how are you adjusting?

Studies have shown that transracially adopted children sometimes identify with their parents' race rather than their own. Culture is passed on by families. Transracial adoption is perhaps one of the most controversial issues discussed by social workers for this very reason. Many social workers, especially the National Association of Black Social Workers, oppose transracial adoptions. Black children need to be with black parents, they say, because only African-American parents can teach their children how to handle racism. What do you think? Is there any truth to this? Does this mean that children in foster care should remain there until parents of the right color come along? California lawmakers think so. A new California law, which went into effect in January 1990, requires foster care agencies to spend ninety days trying to match children ethnically before allowing transracial placement.

It's a tough issue. Is it better for children to wait—for months or years—for the perfect family, or is it better to be placed transracially in a loving home? According to statistics, about forty to fifty percent of all foster children are black. There are many of biracial parentage.

"Should race be the only issue looked at, especially when there is no other family available to adopt that child?" asks Lynette Popejoy, who is the white mother of four children, three of whom are black and one is biracial. "Our daughter came to us in two months whereas we would have had to wait twelve months if the baby were white. We were thrilled to have her; she was ours whether I gave birth to her or not. She was ours whether she 'matched' us or not. She was ours."

Lynette and her husband adopted Emily, a newborn, in 1985. They immediately got the same treatment that some interracial families receive from their extended family: isolation.

But she and her military husband wanted more children. To their advantage, they were already parents to a minority child. They went through the adoption process three more times.

"Social workers had more justification placing other black children with us," says Popejoy. "They thought we walked on water. It wasn't a negative issue to do that. But things have changed a lot since then. Today, black social workers believe it's best to wait for black families to place these children with.

"If there's no family waiting for that child, I don't

see keeping that child in a foster home, waiting," she continues. "I found kids who had been in the system for years, but when we presented our family saying 'Yes, we would love to have that child,' the social workers said, 'Yes, but you're not black.'"

Now separated from her husband, Popejoy has found the need for more outside support. She says adopting children from the same race has made it easier for the children to cope. Although they are still very young, the oldest being eight, they have each other. Although Popejoy continues to find support through national adoption groups who put her in contact with other moms and families like hers, she realizes she needs more help.

For example, sometimes her daughter Emily says things like, "I wish I had hair like yours."

It's a very small thing. But for Emily it's a big deal. Caring for Emily's hair is a challenge for Popejoy, whose own hair is of a different texture. Hair care is an issue many biracial teens, especially of black/white heritage, talk about as one of their biggest challenges.

Regent Street Hair Salon owner Gerry Watkins says that because hair comes in so many textures (black hair alone has more than forty different textures), it would be difficult for him to give advice. However, he was able to make some general observations, since his Scottsdale, Arizona, salon serves a wide variety of clients of varying racial backgrounds and hair textures.

Watkins says the best thing to do is seek out a professional hair stylist who specializes in black hair, for advice. During the consultation, the stylist will examine your hair closely, feeling the texture of your hair wet and dry, ask you questions about your current hair care treatment and how your hair responds to it, and make recommendations on products and styles. Consultations are usually free, even at very expensive shops, he added.

But Emily has other, more pressing concerns than her hair. The kids at school were calling her "brown." Her mother sees that Emily's race is slowly becoming an issue, and Emily is in need of minority coping skills that Popejoy can't offer.

"I tell her she's an attractive child, and I talk about my own childhood and of being teased. I told her that the best option is to not react to it and that boys like to tease girls. But I don't know how to handle it really."

But she's learning. Popejoy brings home books on African-American history to share with her children. She's joined her state chapter of the National Association for the Advancement of Colored People. She plans on taking the children to black churches. Although she lives in a predominantly white neighborhood, there is a multiracial family across the street.

Adoption is a very beautiful thing. It gives a second chance to both the children and the persons adopting them. Some people can be very insensitive, asking inappropriate questions. Why? Because it's not what they're used to. Following are a few tips your adopted mother or father can pass along to those probing folks to keep them from making the same mistake twice:

- Don't make remarks or ask questions about real parents. The child's adopted family are real parents, grandparents, aunts, uncles, etc.
- Don't ask why the birth parents didn't want their child—especially in front of the child. They may have wanted him or her very much, but have been forced by circumstance to give their child up for adoption.

• Don't ask how much a child cost. The child cost nothing. There were legal, medical, and agency fees. But asking how much is terribly rude.
• A school teacher shouldn't ask students to make a family tree. Chances are, there is an adopted child in the class or ones from divorced or blended families.
• And finally, don't ask adoptive parents who their child looks like. How are they supposed to know?

Let's close this chapter with a poem written by Popejoy about the adoption process.

> FOR THE VERY SPECIAL KIDS
> You begin looking thru the big, heavy book
> You are taken in by each sad but sweet look
> You read about their pasts and difficult start
> Like a seed, each one begins to grow in your heart
> You wonder how many you are able to feed
> As you turn the pages and continue to read
> You take the social worker's numbers and start to
>   call
> Wondering how you'll accept not taking them all
> Intently you listen to the social worker's word
> It is hard to believe all you have just heard
> The pain and the suffering these kids have been
>   thru
> To hold back the tears is all you can do
> They have been waiting for a mom and dad for so
>   long
> The society who lets this all happen is wrong
> Your homestudy goes out to so many places
> At night when you dream you see each of their
>   faces

After many delays your child is home
But you still worry about the ones left alone
You bonded with your new child from the moment
   you met
He has found a new family, but he hasn't realized
   yet
Soon he starts to look you right in the eyes
Those stories of him being hopeless were all lies
You have taught him to laugh, to sing and to play
He turns to you with a smile and says that he'll
   stay
You can hardly believe when he calls you mom
   and dad
Yet you know inside why you are a little bit sad
So back to the books you go that very day
To bring another very special child home to stay.

CHAPTER 8

The Best of Both

Worlds

The most difficult aspect of being biracial is perhaps also the best part: having more than one race or culture to identify with. That seems to be the prevailing attitude among teens with multicultural backgrounds and their parents. In this culturally diverse society, you're the only one who can really celebrate true racial harmony. You're living proof; you possess the best of both worlds.

Following is a story about a twenty-three-year-old biracial woman. Looking at her dark features and pale, silky skin, you would think she was Greek or Italian. The only thing you can tell for sure from her appearance is that she is very beautiful. Her name is Nancie Parra. She's a graduate of Arizona State University, where she received a degree in political science. Nancie was excited when she heard about this book, and without being asked for comments, she said she was happy to be biracial. She had the best of both worlds, she said. Here is her story, in her own words.

"I am the product of an interracial marriage. My father is Mexican, born and raised in Mexico where he played professional baseball. He didn't complete his education until he married my mom and moved to the United States. His life had been extremely different from my mother's.

"My mom was born in Ellensberg, Washington. She is white. She lived most of her life on college campuses or around schools because both of her parents were educators. She graduated from college and became a teacher. She was on a trip when she met my father at a hotel they were both staying at in Pueblo, Mexico. They married shortly thereafter, even though neither one could really speak the other's language. It was love at first sight. I came along two years later.

"I was born in Pueblo, Mexico, where my mom taught at a private school, and my dad traveled and played baseball. We moved to the United States when I was only three or four. We lived in a border town for a little while. Then we moved to the Phoenix area, where my mom had been given a teaching job and my dad worked at a manufacturing company. The community where we lived was fairly mixed—half and half—with Hispanics and whites. When I started school is when I realized I was different from the majority of kids I went to school with. I really didn't look like either my mother or my father. My mom is blonde with hazel eyes and a fair complexion while my father was the exact opposite: dark hair and with a dark complexion. I'm somewhere in between the two of them.

"I can't remember the first time I realized my mom and I weren't the same. However, I do remember that from very early in school kids teased and called me a half-breed. Well, I never took it to heart or even realized it was anything bad until I was older. My parents had always taught me that I was lucky to have such a diverse background. I was always happy to tell people where I was born. As I got older, probably from about the third grade to the eighth grade, it was more and more difficult for me to identify with a specific group. At my school, the Hispanic kids hung around together and the white kids hung around together. I leaned more toward the white group because they were more from the same economic background. Also, they lived in my neighborhood. This made the Hispanic kids resentful, not to mention the fact that I was also a teacher's kid. The Hispanic girls, especially, were very hateful. They couldn't understand me. I was supposed to be like them, but I wasn't. This was hard for me. I wanted to belong with everyone, but I didn't. My mother's parents along with my parents gave me privileges that other kids in my area—both white and Hispanic—didn't have. I traveled to Europe and went to plays with my grandfather who was a drama professor at California State Fresno. I rarely spent a summer at home like other kids I knew. That was a hard time for me. I always knew I was going to go on to college when the majority of kids I knew were wondering if they were going to graduate from high school.

"Not fitting in is the norm for teenagers, I know that. When I was in high school, the groups were still separated. I didn't associate much with the Hispanic groups. My friends were all white, all born in the United States, and all having both parents who were born here as well as probably their parents before them. I wouldn't say that all their families were prejudiced, but the majority had some feelings against anyone who wasn't like them. During these years, I was exposed to all sorts of prejudice, mainly because I didn't appear to be a minority. Everything from racial slurs and comments to complete racial hatred were a part of my experience. For a time, I was silent and never said a word. That didn't last long. I became very vocal about how offensive I thought people's comments and racial jokes were. But I was always told: 'We don't mean you.' That was the hardest part of being biracial and still is.

"Even in college where things were supposed to be open and intellectual, the same attitudes continued. Surprisingly enough, even the Hispanic groups on campus treated me the way every other Hispanic group I was in contact with treated me: like I didn't belong because I was only half Mexican and that I couldn't possible know or feel the same way they felt about racial prejudice. This is the only real problem about being biracial.

"It's not a problem about knowing who you are and where you came from. But it's other people who can't fit you into a category. My parents raised me to be proud of who I am, and I am proud of my heritage. The benefits of having two cultures far outweigh anything bad I experienced in growing up. We live in a society of many races and cultures. I feel like I have a better understanding of the world. I plan to raise my own children to know and understand their heritage."

Nanci advises only these three things to biracial teens: be proud of your background; focus on building self-esteem so you'll be happy with who you are; and finally, concentrate on making everything equal, race being a secondary consideration.

Now meet the Wade family: Jill and Micah and their three daughters, Mycah, Sarah, and Leah. Jill is white, Micah is black. In 1993, they celebrated their 20th wedding anniversary. Says Micah, "Most of the people who told us not to get married are no longer together."

To concerns voiced twenty years ago about their marriage and the effect it would have on their children, Jill and Micah responded, "What about them?" They were in love. They wanted to be married. Today, twenty years and three daughters later, they are the kind of nuclear family story books are made of. One of Leah's friends called them the Brady Bunch. It's that kind of near-perfect existence between this mom, dad, and three teenage daughters.

Jill is a cool mom. On the weekends, she gives her pager to the girls so that their friends can contact them (and so can she). She is tall, about five feet, nine inches tall, and very attractive. Micah is a Bill Cosby/Cliff Huxtable father, teasing his daughters about their baggy, gangster attire and teen lingo. He's a soft-spoken, educated, professional black man who's kept his ties to the black community. The three girls are as tall as their parents. Mycah and Sara have long, dark manes. Leah's hair is a lighter shade, almost auburn. Although their cover-girl looks draw attention from passersby, they are very natural down-to-earth people.

According to Jill, she and her husband are raising their daughters to have the coping skills of minority people. To raise them as white would do them a disservice because society would view them and treat them as minorities, says Micah. Jill relies on Micah to teach these skills to their daughters. Answering race questions on forms in school, Mycah and Leah often check black. Sarah checks both, but often gets scolded for it. They all agree that a biracial male has it tougher than a female.

For them, support comes from their parents and from each other. They laugh when asked about talking to their high school counselor. "Who is our counselor?" Sarah asks. Teenagers whose parents aren't as open and communicative as Jill and Micah should seek out counselors to confide in. They are the lifeblood for some teens. The Wade sisters have each other.

"I don't know what I would do if I were an only child," says Sarah. "I have my sisters. We can talk to each other." The younger girls look to their older sister Mycah for an example. At age eighteen, she's been where they're going. Right now, they're all attending the same high school; they can shield each other when necessary. Mycah is also ahead of them on the path to the realities of the larger society, where attitudes are much different, and sometimes less accepting. Only their mom is a little nervous.

"It's not that big a deal to me," says Mycah. "I know it is for some people, but I'm not in anguish about it. Oh, no, I'm biracial! I mean, what's the big deal?" That's her attitude. She's always had it. She's confident and articulate. Her belief in herself and her heritage is stronger than prejudice. She's relying on her mental toughness. It's worked so far.

A few problems that they've had have come from other minorities and the prejudiced views of Leah's boyfriend's parents. Sarah has had a strained relationship with African-American girls. "One time they walked behind me and Mycah and were saying stuff right behind us. 'Look at Sarah, she's a white girl.'" Sarah doesn't respond. She hates animosity. "I want to be friends with everyone," she says. "I really go out of my way so they can get to know me." It's worked for her.

Mycah also wants to be friends with everyone at their racially mixed school but is hesitant about going out of her way to do so. "I feel, if they don't want to be friends with me because I'm biracial, I'll just stay away from them. I don't want to be friends with them, either!" She advises teenagers to just be themselves.

Mycah, Sarah, and Leah are not sheltered. They are well aware that things are going to be different when they let go of Mom's apron strings and they're on their own. Sarah would like to go to an all-black college, but worries about having to start all over again in gaining acceptance from her black contemporaries.

Leah, very shy, once told her mom that she was glad to be biracial. Why? Because she would fit in with both white people and black people. "When I'm with white friends, I feel like I'm white and I fit in," she says. "When I'm with black girls, I feel like I fit in too."

Walking through a city festival, Jill, Mycah, and Sarah walk with arms locked around each other. Leah and her father walk hand-in-hand close by. This picture says to others: We're proud to have the best of both worlds.

Following is the Wade family's story, in their own words:

Jill

"My name is Jill Marie Wade and my husband's name is Micah. We have been married for twenty years and we have three daughters: Mycah Marie, Sarah Summer, and Leah Lynn. They are eighteen, fifteen, and fourteen years old respectively. I am white, mostly of German descent, and Micah is black, mostly of African and Indian descent. I was raised in an almost completely white environment. In fact, I didn't go to school with someone of African descent until I was in high school, and then there was only one black student in a school of over 3,000 students.

"I met Micah while he was in Phoenix attending college. We dated secretly for one year. When we announced our plans to marry, much to the dismay of my parents, we moved to California to live. Micah's family lived in the San Francisco Bay area, and even though his family had doubts about our marriage, they supported and accepted me into the family. Mycah was born almost two years into our marriage. When she was two years old, we moved back to Arizona, as my mother was very sick, and Micah had a nice job offer from a large corporation in Phoenix. By this time, my parents had accepted my marriage to Micah. My mother actually had developed a close relationship with Micah. My father treated him as a son, and since they had similar interests their relationship naturally grew as well.

"When the girls were very young, I was too busy to think about how they would interact in the outside world. However, as they approached the school years, I began to think that they needed to develop their own identities. It made sense to me that as I had no practical experience in being a minority, the logical thing to do was ask Micah to teach the children coping skills. Micah and I believed that the girls should be raised to see themselves as a minority as this would give them something concrete to begin with. I truly believe that we made the right decision, as all three of my girls are very well adjusted and they have friends of all colors."

Mycah

"I never think of myself as being different when I am with a group of people unless someone says something. Then I'm taken aback, and I think, 'Oh, so you see me THAT WAY!' This doesn't happen very often, as I just try to get along with everyone and I have friends that are white, black, Mexican, and Asian. I have had boyfriends who were both black and white in the past, and I do not really think about what they are when I meet them. I just either am interested in them or not! I think that by having both of my parents raise me together, I feel comfortable with all races. I'm very happy to be biracial, and so far I've had very few problems because of it. Mostly, I have had good experiences."

Sarah

"The only group of people that I seem to get bad vibes from are African-American girls. For some reason before they've had the chance to get to know me, they have an attitude toward me like they think that I think that I'm too cute. Usually when this happens, for example, at a new school, I seek those girls out and try to get to know them. Sure enough, they end up being good friends with me, or at least people who will say 'Hi' to me when I pass by them. Last year when I was in track, it gave me the chance to get to know several of the black girls that I didn't know before. This was a good opportunity for them to see me as I really am. I am mostly attracted to black guys, although I have had white boyfriends before. As I look more African-American than my sisters, it's possible that I attract African-American boys more often. As all three of us attend the same high school, we have a lot of the same friends. Ironically, we have several friends who are also bi-racial. In fact, we went to a retreat last year that was designed to make everyone aware of the many races. Mycah and I were invited to go so that there would be enough biracial kids there to make up a separate group for some of the exercises. It was a very emotional weekend, and I believe everyone that went came home with a new appreciation for the other races."

Leah

"I *LOVE* being biracial. I understand and get along with both races. When I am with my father's family, I laugh and understand their humor and their problems. And when I'm with my mother's family, I laugh and understand them too! I think that I get the best of both worlds. I had boyfriends back in the third and fourth grades, and they were usually white. But now I'm in the ninth grade and I have my first real boyfriend; he's black. We both play basketball. Basketball is my first love, and really I just go and play the game without really thinking about racial things. When I do think about it, I realize that I am out there playing with girls of every race, and we are having a great time! Most of the girls I hang out with are white. In fact, my best friend is white, but I also have girlfriends that are black and Mexican."

Micah

"I was raised in Alameda, California. That is a mainly white community in northern California. My mother was active in the National Association for the Advancement of Colored People (NAACP), holding the president's position for many years. She was adept in dealing with business persons of all races, and I believe my brothers and sisters and I learned this from her. As my family was about the only black family on the island of Alameda, we had to deal with a lot of prejudice. However, as most minorities eventually do, we all learned how to get along with the white kids and eventually we gained acceptance. This ability is second nature to me now. I believe it has been a major factor in raising my girls with the flexibility they now seem to have in getting along with others.

"I just felt that my girls would have all the tools they needed to succeed in life if they would see themselves as I saw myself, as a child. In this world, I believe I would be doing a disservice to my children if I did not give them an identity as *EVERYONE* in *EVERY FORM* wants to know: *WHAT ARE YOU?* If my girls tried to be accepted as white, I felt that this would only be setting them up for criticism, frustration, and maybe more problems than that. This is a cruel world, and in general, the African-American people are more accepting of persons that are of mixed race as this has been a part of our culture for years! This has proved to be true, and I have made an interesting observation. All three of my girls look different and could actually pass for many different races. However, it seems that whenever they are approached by an African-American, I would say ninety-eight percent of the time, the person will know that they have African-American blood in them. Yet, any other person of any other race will not be able to guess even part of their ancestry with any degree of accuracy."

The Wade family. The best of both worlds.

CHAPTER ◊ 9

You're Not Alone

How does a biracial teenager grow up to be a happy, healthy adult? By having an excellent support structure.

One word that has been used over and over throughout this book is: support. Although you may feel that you're all alone in your struggle to find an identity and integrate into a society obsessed with color and categorizing its members, you're not. You're not alone. You have your family. There are also more than twenty-five books you can read, more than fifty interracial groups across the country to join, hundreds of articles to read, and more than five million other biracial individuals in this country to talk to. These things are the focus of this chapter.

Parents can give their children the gift of self-esteem by making sure they have toys and books that reflect their own experiences and racial backgrounds. You might be too old for toys, but perhaps your little brother and sister aren't. Remember, your family is going to be your strongest support system. When was the last time you were in a toy store? Did you know that an increasing number of doll manufacturers are producing dolls with not an ethnic look, but a biracial look? Mattel Toys Shani line includes three beautifully attired dolls designed to represent light, mid-brown, and dark-brown skin. Huggy Bean, a tan doll with long hair, allows biracial children to cuddle up with a baby doll that looks like them. Hearthsong catalog features a kit for making a wheat-colored doll with dark hair. Progress still needs to be made in the area for little boys, but this is a great start.

Books are a great avenue for teenagers like yourself to use. And they don't have to be adult books either. Take a look at the reading list at the end of this book.

Outside of books, there are support groups for you and your parents to join. You will find that many of the support groups are nonprofit; they sponsor programs and activities for individuals and families; they publish their own newsletters; they have membership fees that include monthly mailings; and they are open to anyone. You and your parents can write to the ones in your area that best fit your family's needs. Your family may want to start your own if there isn't one in your town. You can also start one in your school. Chapter 3 provided you with a few pointers on starting a support group, but do write to the established organizations for information. The point is: There's a wealth of information and support out there. Most of these organizations were started in the living rooms of concerned parents or in a school where racial tension had run its course. A few of the many groups are listed in the Help List.

Along with local support, many of these groups can provide information about which neighborhoods and schools are integrated and hospitable to interracial families. This would be very valuable information if your family were relocating to a new state. You would have instant friends who are concerned about your adjusting to a new environment. Members of these groups also share ideas about creating toys, books, games, and educational materials that reflect their children's biracial identity.

New People is a magazine targeted for "everyone who sees the world not as color-conscious, but color full." Produced in Oak Park, Michigan, *New People* includes articles on transracial adoption, interracial dating, and interracial family issues, and it even boasts an interracial comic strip, "It Figures." For $1, they will mail you an updated list of interracial groups, or you can order a magazine subscription for $15 a year.

If nothing else, being an active member of a support group will give you an opportunity to be in a positive environment, surrounded by individuals and families with similar needs. To be alone means you are separated from others; isolated, excluding anyone or anything else. Just look around; you're really not alone. The next time someone inquires, "What are you?" tell them your racial identity with pride, and also tell them that you're not alone.

People should be able to celebrate all parts of their heritage without conflict. Interracial marriages that work produce multiracial children at ease with their mixed identity, which in turn produces more people in the world who can deal with diversity. The peoples of the world have much to learn about living with diversity.

CHAPTER 10

One Last Word

Being a biracial teenager (no matter what racial or ethnic heritage you have) will probably mean that you have to face the following: living in the world of one race while always on guard to defend yourself against slurs from the other; feeling as if you have disappointed one of your parents because you resemble people of your other parent's race; and wanting to be just a person but constantly being reminded that you have to be aware of race. As you begin to grow older and mature and seek out your own answers, you'll continue to cope better and better.

Your parent or parents hopefully are comfortable with their own cultural heritages, neither exaggerating nor minimizing the differences between them. That will be instrumental in helping you deal with who you are. When children don't feel pressured to choose one race over the other, they learn to embrace both cultures. You also need to realize that racism and prejudice are *social* realities— they are not the reality of your family life. Some interracial families may experience intraracism, racism among their own family members, but those families either try to work out their problems or dissociate themselves from the ones causing problems.

There is a clear difference between what is inside the family and outside. Racism is usually outside. It, along with stereotyping, can lead to your discomfort and confusion about your identity if it's not talked about immediately. For example, Asian-Americans are a very diverse group—many of them were born and acculturated in Asia; and many of them are American-born, knowing no language other than English. Yet, many Asian-Americans are seen as Asian first and only, although they are from Asian-American/white unions. A teenager from this background is most likely entirely American in culture. But that doesn't make a difference to some people. You probably know some of them. They'll ask these teenagers if they know karate or are good in math. Teachers may ask them to show the other students how to write some Chinese or Japanese characters. Can you see how teenagers subjected to this and to name-calling can be uncomfortable are ashamed of their Asian-American identity?

According to those who have grown up with Asian-American heritage, there are two extremes of identity development. The first involves the complete denial of one's Asian background. This teenager may avoid other Asians and try very hard to impress upon other people his or her complete Americanness. This is the so-called banana response (yellow on the outside, white on the inside) that some Asians are labeled by other Asians. The other extreme can involve a radical Asian-only identification. This teenager may completely reject the values of the dominant American culture.

These two forms of identity development may come about in those of other mixed heritages as well. No race or ethnic group is immune to racism and its effects. Luckily, the potential damage that racism can cause can be prevented. Parents can instill a sense of pride in their children in a number of ways. Among these are to foster the children's contacts with relatives and friends of their different racial or ethnic group. They should especially promote exposure to other children in these groups; after all, you're half like them. It is also important for you to be able to identify racism so its negative images won't be incorporated into your developing self-concept. Do you know other teenagers within the ethnic groups you belong to? Can you identify racism when you experience it? Do you talk to a parent or an adult about your feelings?

Communication really is the key to growing up healthy in an interracial family. Parents need to talk to their children early on and throughout their lives. Teenagers should talk to their parents. Siblings should talk to other siblings. Teenagers should talk to other teenagers like them or to their parents if their own are not willing or able. As long as you're talking, you're growing up healthy.

Every culture seems to relay the same message: Parents must help you develop a positive self-image and pride in your identity by dealing with your racial and cultural differences. This should be an on-going discussion in which you participate. Hopefully, your parent presents both cultures with equal respect and discuss both cultures fully— their positive and negative aspects, their complexities, their contradictions, and the ambivalent feelings they may generate.

It is also important to look openly at cultural attitudes toward intermarriage. What is the unwritten law within the culture? How have people usually responded? Are these feelings likely to change? Many biracial and bicultural families have the added problem of isolation as their friends and families often have difficulty accepting a person from another cultural background.

Raising healthy children in our society is a very difficult task. Gone are the days of "Leave it to Beaver," a situation comedy in which crossing the street was the biggest danger for kids. Gone are towns like Mayberry, where the deputy carries an unloaded pistol. Gone are the days when gum-chewing was the biggest concern for classroom teachers.

Teenagers often want clear-cut answers: How do I cope? There's no one answer, but rather a combination of everything that has been discussed in this book. Here are some recaps:

- The degree of racism experienced usually depends on what features and skin color you have, where you live, parental influence and support.
- Environment will often determine how you feel about yourself; if you feel accepted, chances are you're provided with confidence and pride in your unique diversity; if the environment is more hostile (angry), you'll display hostility and withdraw.
- The pressure is strong to belong to both your ethnic groups, but sometimes features and skin tones won't let you.
- Within one family, siblings may choose separate races based on what they look like.
- Biracial kids learn to answer the questions about their family before they're asked.
- You can have anything you want as long as you understand yourself.
- You'll feel comfortable around people of many different racial and ethnic backgrounds.

- You probably are less tolerant of racial jokes than most of your friends.
- There are many support groups available for you and your family. You can start your own if there isn't one in your area.
- Society is beginning to recognize the need to include multiethnic Americans in literature.
- By the middle of the twenty-first century, all current racial categories in America will become almost meaningless. Minority groups will be the majority.
- Passing as someone you're not is your choice. Pride and honesty are the real challenges.
- Life is tough for all teenagers. The more you seek out information, the better growing up will be for you.
- Love and compatibility are the major reasons for most interracial relationships. Chances are, you are not a product of an unhealthy union. Listening to people who think otherwise will only cause you emotional damage.
- Educate others. How else will they know if you don't educate them.
- You are somebody. You have a place. Your unique diverse heritage is positive.

And finally, take with you the words of one multiethnic American: "Bicultural, biracial families play a very important role in today's world. With hatred, fear, and oppression of others the order of the day, we can become models of a truly peaceful and creative coexistence."

Help List

Support Groups

NATIONAL

Association of MultiEthnic Americans
P.O. Box 191726
San Francisco, CA 94119-1726
510/523-AMEA

Association for Multicultral Counseling and Development
5999 Stevenson Avenue
Alexandria, VA 22304

Project Race
1425 Market Boulevard
Roswell, GA 30076
404/640-7100

ARMED FORCES

Multicultural Family Support Group
Attn: Ken and Chuck Berg
466-4 West Reckord Ave.
Fort Ritchie, MD 21719

THE SOUTH

Interracial Family Circle
P.O. Box 53290
Washington, DC 20009
703/719-9887

Interracial Family Alliance
P.O. Box 20290
Atlanta, GA 30325
404/696-8113

THE NORTHEAST

Council on Interracial Books for Children
1841 Broadway
New York, NY 10023
212/757-5339

THE MIDWEST

Biracial Family Network
P.O. Box 3214
Chicago, IL 60654
312/921-1335

THE WEST

Interracial Intercultural Pride (I-Pride)
P.O. Box 191752
San Francisco, CA 94119-1752
415/399-9111

Glossary

affiliation   Association, relationship.

census   An offical count of the population, often with classified social and economic statistics.

complacent   Unconcerned, not watchful.

component   Part.

contemporary   living, occurring, or existing at the same time.

culture   An act of developing by education, discipline, or training.

discounted   Dismissed, ignored, considered to have little value.

diversity   Variety.

ethnicity   Of, pertaining to, or designating races or groups of races on the basis of common traits, customs, etc.

integrate   To become one with, to unite.

hospitable   Friendly, welcoming.

outmoded   Out of style.

phase   Condition or stage in which change takes place.

race   An implied biological distinction between groups of people.

relay   To pass on from one to another.

status   Where one stands in relation to others.

transracial   Across racial lines.

For Futher Reading

Easy Reading

Miles, Betty. *All it Takes Is Practice*. New York: Knopf, 1976.

Adoff, Arnold. *All the Colors of the Race*. New York: Lothrop, 1982.

———. *Black Is Brown Is Tan*. New York: Harper & Row, 1973.

Bode, Janet. *Different Worlds: Interracial and Cross-Cutural Dating*. New York: Franklin Watts, 1989.

Jones, Adrienne. *So Nothing Is Forever*. New York: Houghton-Mifflin, 1974.

Almonte, Paul, and Desmond, Theresa. *The Facts about Interracial Marriage*. New York: Crestwood House, 1992.

Williams, Garth. *The Rabbits' Wedding*. New York: Harper & Row, 1958.

Gay, Kathlyn. *The Rainbow Effect: Interracial Families*. New York: Franklin Watts, 1987.

Welber, Robert. *The Train*. New York: Pantheon, 1972.

Challenging Reading

Mathabane, Gail and Mathabane, Mark. *Love in Black and White: The Triumph of Love Over Prejudice and Taboo*. New York: HarperCollins, 1992.

Day, Beth. *Sexual Life Between Blacks and Whites: The Roots of Racism*. New York: World Publishing, Times Mirror, 1972.

Index